# The Mystical Meaning of Dreams

Rabbi Avraham

A TARGUM PRESS Book

First published 2006
Copyright © 2006 by Avraham Arieh Trugman
ISBN 1-56871-400-9

Published by:
TARGUM PRESS, INC.
22700 W. Eleven Mile Rd.
Southfield, MI 48034
E-mail: targum@netvision.net.il
Fax: 888-298-9992
www.targum.com

Distributed by:
FELDHEIM PUBLISHERS
208 Airport Executive Park
Nanuet, NY 10954

Printing plates by Frank, Jerusalem
Printed in Israel by Chish

# Rav Zev Leff

*Rabbi of Moshav Mattityahu*

*Rosh Hayeshiva Yeshiva Gedola Matisyahu*

D.N. Modi'in 71917 Tel. (08) 976-1138 Fax. (08) 976-5326

16 Menachem Av 5765

Dear Friends,

I have read the manuscript of *The Mystical Meaning of Dreams* by my friend and colleague Rabbi Avraham Arieh Trugman. As in his previous books, Rabbi Trugman weaves an interesting combination of basic Torah sources and their traditional commentaries with Chassidic and Kabbalistic nuances along with scientific information to shed light on the makeup of dreams and their significance.

He studies the various dreams mentioned in Tanach, especially the dream of Yaakov Avinu of the ladder spanning heaven and earth, and illuminates them with the understanding of our Sages to reveal the components and sources of the various types of dreams.

I have found this word to be interesting, informative, and based on sound Torah sources and recommend it as a source for understanding the concept of dreams from a Torah perspective. I commend Rabbi Trugman for extending his work in disseminating Torah to the masses, especially reaching out to those estranged from Judaism, with illuminating works such as this. May Hashem grant him and his family life, health, and strength to continue to merit the community.

With Torah blessings,

Rabbi Zev Leff

# Rabbi Yitzchak Ginsburgh

*Gal Einai Institute* P.O. Box 1015, *Kfar Chabad* 72915, Israel

To my dear student HaRav Avraham Arieh Trugman,

*Shalom u'vracha*!

I was very happy to receive your new book *The Mystical Meaning of Dreams*. I enjoyed greatly reading it and want to bless you with much success in publishing and distributing the book. It should be His will that the book should arouse the inner Divine spark in many Jews and through this the dream of the generations — the true and consummate redemption by our righteous *Mashiach* — will be quickly realized.

It is known that Yosef the Tzaddik is the "master of dreams." He is the master of all matters relating to dreams both as the one who dreams dreams (real dreams that in the future will be realized) and also as the interpreter of others' dreams. In Kabbalah, Yosef corresponds to the *sefirah* of foundation, of which it said: "The tzaddik [the righteous one] is the foundation of the world." The *sefirah* of foundation is the mark of the holy covenant that receives the living and viable seed from the two *sefirot* victory and acknowledgment (which ripen the seed). In the introduction to the *Tikunei Zohar*, victory and acknowledgment are described as the root of the souls of the Prophets and visionaries of Israel. The secret of the three *sefirot* victory, acknowledgment, and foundation is thus the secret of the true dreamer of dreams who also receives from the root of the Prophets and visionaries.

From the power of his father Jacob (the archetypal soul of the *sefirah* of beauty, which corresponds to the vowel sign *cholam*, as explained in your book), Yosef — who dreams the dream of his own life —

draws down the seminal dream of redemption for the people of Israel and the entire world to the *sefirah* of kingdom, which represents the entire communal aspect of the people of Israel.

It follows therefore that the clarification of the dreams dreamt by each and every man and woman of the people of Israel is dependent on their connection to the true tzaddik — the Yosef — of the generation.

May it be the Almighty's will that we all merit to connect to the true *tzaddik* and through this merit to see the fulfillment of the verse: "And to Zion [the innermost point of the heart of every Jew] will come a redeemer." That is, that the tzaddik of the generation will merit to be the M*ashiach* in actuality, and through this manifest the dream of all the generations. Amen! May it be the Almighty's will speedily in our lifetime.

From the one who always seeks your peace,

Yitzchak Ginsburgh

This book
is dedicated to
the loving memory of

# Chaim ben
# R' Yechiel Dov Ber, *z"l*

May it be for a blessing.

To our granddaughter,

**Batya Tzofia Nechama
bat Ben Tzion Arieh Moshe and Miriam**,

who was born on Tishah B'Av.

She represents our awed expectation, *Tzofia*, of
rebuilding the Temple in our time, *Nechama*.

Sara and Henoch Dov Hoffman

In honor of the wedding of

**Daphna Brandt**
(דפנה אודיה בת טוביה בער)
and
**Ben Kapnik**
(יחיאל בנימין בן שמחה שעיה)

May their dreams always bring them closer
and guide them together with
love of God and Torah.

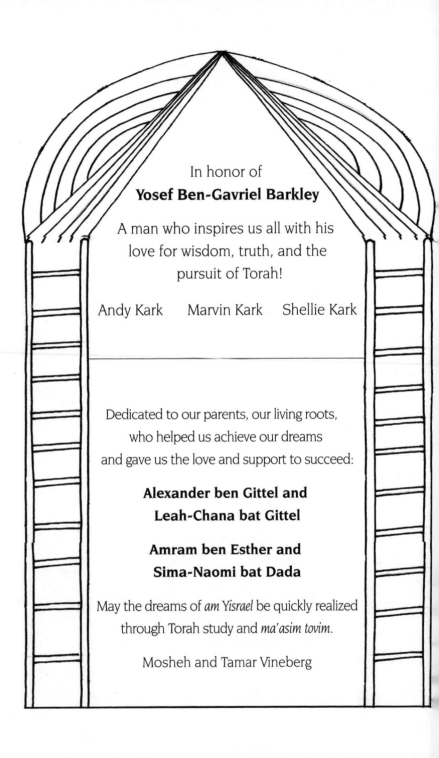

In honor of
**Yosef Ben-Gavriel Barkley**

A man who inspires us all with his
love for wisdom, truth, and the
pursuit of Torah!

Andy Kark    Marvin Kark    Shellie Kark

Dedicated to our parents, our living roots,
who helped us achieve our dreams
and gave us the love and support to succeed:

**Alexander ben Gittel and
Leah-Chana bat Gittel**

**Amram ben Esther and
Sima-Naomi bat Dada**

May the dreams of *am Yisrael* be quickly realized
through Torah study and *ma'asim tovim*.

Mosheh and Tamar Vineberg

# Table of Contents

# Acknowledgments

Writing a book is like a dream coming true. It begins as a vague collection of ideas, passing thoughts, and sparks of inspiration, which slowly come together and finally crystallize into a complete book. Throughout that process many people play their part in helping make the dream real.

I would first and foremost like to thank Rabbi Moshe Dombey, *z"l*, the head of Targum Press, who passed away during the final stages of preparing this book for publication. He was many things to many people, but most of all he was a true mensch. You could always be sure you were getting the true picture from him and his word was like gold. He was instrumental in publishing all three of my books and will be sorely missed.

I would like to thank the wonderful staff of Targum Press, especially Chaya Baila Gavant for her superb editing skills; Diane Liff for the overall layout and her insightful input into the cover, the inside design, and the best way to use my drawings; and Miriam Zakon for her advice in shaping the original concept of this book.

I want to express deep gratitude to Rabbi Shlomo Carlebach, who not only taught me how to dream, but also inspired me to actualize those dreams.

Special acknowledgment goes to Rabbi Yitzchak Ginsburgh, from whom I've been privileged to learn for over thirty years and whose teachings are quoted throughout this book. Your blessings and encouragement have been a source of ongoing strength and inspiration.

Heartfelt thanks to Rabbi Zev Leff who has graciously reviewed all my books and written beautiful approbations for them. Your keen insight was very valuable in the editing stage of this book.

Many thanks to those whose dedications helped bring this book into being: Andy, Marvin, and Shellie Kark; Mosheh and Tamar Vineberg; Rabbi Henoch Dov and Sari Hoffman; and Tuvia and Jayne Brandt. Please know how much I appreciate your assistance in realizing this project.

I want to take this opportunity to acknowledge the following ongoing supporters of Ohr Chadash, whose generosity allows us to bring the light of Torah to an ever-growing constituency:

- Very special thanks to Marty and Chavi Lee, whose friendship and support of Ohr Chadash has been our foundation stone from day one. May you continue to get much *nachas* as Ohr Chadash grows.

- To Barbara and Michael Katch, good friends of many years, for believing in the work we do and becoming true partners with us in such a generous and loving manner.

- To George and Sheera Gumbiner, Scott and Sally Alpert, and Alain and Deborah Sutton — for your ongoing generosity and trusting support. I can't thank you enough.

- And to Alan and Lori Lurie, Chuck and Betty Whiting, Michael and Barbara Schwartz, Zvi and Sharon Gelt, Rabbi Henoch Dov and Sari Hoffman, Jeffrey and Shelly Cohen, Steven Alevy, Ivan and Barbara Geller, Walter Goldberg, Nate and Amy Davidovich, Ken and Vickie Pepper, and Fred and Karen Pasternack, thank you for helping make Ohr Chadash a reality.

To my wife Rachel and my children and their families — you are what dreams are all about. May we share each other's lives and dreams for many years to come.

And above all to the Ribbono shel Olam, the Master of the World, whose kindness endures forever. May I merit to dream and to envision Your dream for the world.

# Introduction

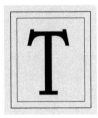hey inspire us and frighten us, amuse us and bewilder us. They make a lasting impression, yet we are liable to forget them in a split second. They are at times mysterious and enigmatic, colorful and fantastic, yet at other times ridiculous, bothersome, and illogical. They have changed the course of history, caused rulers to rise and fall from power, and revealed the future to prophets, kings, and common people. Dreams are all of the above and much more.

The word "dreamer" is usually a belittling statement, a sign of a lazy personality or one with a tenuous grip on reality. Yet to say that someone has a dream gives the connotation of a visionary who is driven by both idealism and destiny. To dream is to fantasize in the most crude or lofty sense, and this is exactly the paradoxical nature of dreams.

In this book we hope to examine the essence and meaning of dreams — from the practical to the mystical. We will investigate dreams in the context of Jewish tradition, as well as touch on modern ideas developed by psychoanalysis. We will try to understand the source of dreams in the body, mind, and soul of man, and trace the connection of dreaming to the very roots of human consciousness.

A most fascinating subject we will contemplate is the very fine line between subjective and objective; what exactly is a dream state and what constitutes "reality."

We will present ideas of how various dream-like states can be used to not only enrich reality, but to create it as well. Dreams are the substance reality is made of and reality is the fuel feeding the fire of dreams.

In the second part of this book, we will focus on one of the most fascinating dreams of all time — Jacob's dream of angels ascending and descending a ladder that reached the heavens. We will delve into the symbolism behind the various elements of this eternal dream and apply its inner meaning in various ways, from the practical to the mystical.

&.&

In such a short book we can only set before the reader various texts, sources, and ideas in the hope that these will be used to open up new doors of perception and new gates of understanding. It is our greatest desire that you will find these ideas personally useful and relevant, inspiring a new appreciation for the importance of dreams and ultimately motivating a deep inner quest for the mystical meaning of dreams.

# Part I

# The Ladder of Dreams

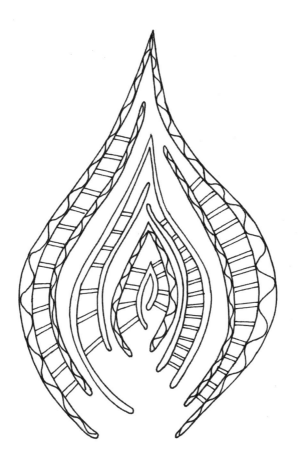

# 1

# Dreams in Jewish Tradition

I n order to understand the significance of dreams in Jewish tradition, we need to begin by examining the topic as presented by the written and oral Torah. Even a superficial study of the essential written and oral texts of Judaism show a rich history and multifaceted discussion of dreams.

In the five books of Moses there are ten incidents in which dreams play a significant role, as well as a number of highly significant events that take place during a state of "deep sleep." All ten dreams occur in the book of Genesis, as do the incidents of "deep sleep." Many of these are among the most famous and beloved of all Biblical stories. Dreams also played a major role in the lives of the judges, kings, and prophets, as recorded in the books of the Prophets and Writings.

The importance of dreams is also expressed throughout the Talmud and Midrash, the main sources of the oral tradition, as well as in Jewish law and Kabbalah, the Jewish mystical tradition.

Although we cannot possibly bring all the various sources mentioned above, we will try to give an overview of many important dreams and of the different teachings on their essential nature.

# The Ten Dreams of Genesis

The main theme underlying all the dreams of Genesis is the notion that dreams are either a channel of Divine inspiration and prophecy or the means through which Divine messages or signs are transmitted to the dreamer. Despite the occasional presence of inner struggles and unconscious psychological pressures, which are classic formulas for understanding the psychological source of dreams and will be discussed in greater depth later in this book, there is no doubt that Biblical dreams are either prophetic in nature or the instrument of Divine intervention.

A beautiful allusion to the connection between dreams and prophecy is seen in the following numerical correspondence. The root of the Hebrew word for "dream" appears forty-eight times in the book of Genesis and another seven times in the other four books of the Pentateuch. These numbers correspond exactly to the statement in the Talmud that there were forty-eight prophets and seven prophetesses who prophesied to Israel (*Megillah* 48a). This numerical correspondence alludes strongly to an essential connection between dreams and prophetic states of consciousness. The Talmud in fact states that dreams are one-sixtieth of prophecy (*Berachot* 57b). This prophetic theme, as portrayed by the ten dreams of Genesis, has no doubt left a major impression on the Jewish people and on the world at large.

Let us now examine the ten dreams in chronological order:

1. When Abraham and Sarah journeyed to Gerar, Abraham told the people there that Sarah was his sister, as he feared that he would be killed so that they could take her from him. The king Abimelech did in fact take her into his house due to her great beauty. God came to Abimelech in "a dream of the night" and warned him that he would die for having taken Sarah, since she was married to Abraham. Abimelech in the dream protests his

innocence, inasmuch as Abraham had said she was his sister. God accepts his defense, but warns him to return Sarah to Abraham immediately or the king and all who are connected to him would die.

When Abimelech awakes in the morning he calls all his servants and tells them of his dream. The Torah relates that they were all very frightened, which teaches us that they all accepted the dream as an authentic message from Heaven needing immediate attention. Abimelech heeded the Divine instruction and returned Sarah to Abraham (Genesis 20:1–17).

2. Perhaps the most eternally symbolic and significant of all the ten dreams is the dream of Jacob, who was escaping his brother Esau and spent the night in Beit-El. While he slept, he saw "a ladder was set in the earth and its head reached the heavens, and behold, angels of God were ascending and descending on it…" (Genesis 28:12). God then speaks to him and promises the Land of Israel to him and to his descendants. So archetypical, prophetic, and pregnant with meaning is Jacob's dream that we have chosen it to be the basis of the second part of this book. We hope to delve into the many different levels of meaning of this dream in great detail there.

3. After having worked for Laban fourteen years, Jacob declares his desire to return with his family to his homeland. For all those years Jacob had worked loyally to build up Laban's wealth, but had nothing personally to show for it. In reply to Laban's offer to name his wage, Jacob responds with a seemingly bizarre plan of dividing the sheep in a way that makes Laban confident he will retain virtually all his wealth, leaving Jacob with nothing. Instead, the Torah describes how Jacob, through a methodical mating ritual, actually transforms all of Laban's flocks to his own.

Later, as Laban turns against Jacob and Jacob prepares to flee, he reveals to Leah and Rachel that an angel of God appeared to him in a dream and showed him how he was destined to take possession of all of Laban's sheep and that the time to return to Israel had come (Genesis 30:25–31:17). The manner in which Jacob transforms the pure white and pure black sheep into "ringed, spotted, and checkered" sheep is full of deep Kabbalistic allusions to the process of Creation and the nature of all material and spiritual reality.

4. After Jacob and his family fled, Laban began to chase after him. As he closed in on Jacob, God appeared to him in a dream and warned him not to speak to Jacob "either good or bad" (Genesis 31:22–24). It is interesting to note that of the ten dreams only those of Abimelech and Laban are termed "a dream by night." This indicates that neither Abimelech nor Laban was worthy of God appearing to him except for the sake of Sarah and Jacob.

5. "These are the generations of Jacob, Joseph..." (Genesis 37:1). In this verse Joseph is singled out among all the sons of Jacob. The Midrash explains that many of the occurrences in the life of Jacob were repeated in the life of Joseph (*Bereishit Rabbah* 84:6). It is from Jacob that Joseph learned the symbolism of dreams and how to interpret them. Just as Jacob dreamt two dreams, so too did Joseph. In his first dream he dreamt of himself and his brothers binding sheaves in the midst of the field, when suddenly his sheaf arose and all of his brothers' sheaves bowed down to his (Genesis 37:5–7).

Whereas Joseph understood the dream in a prophetic manner, his brothers interpreted it as the projection of selfish fantasies and an expression of Joseph's desire to rule over them. The Slonimer Rebbe, Rabbi Shalom Noach Berezovsky, *zt"l*, explains that Joseph shared his dreams with his brothers in the naïve hope that they would accept his dreams as a Divine message of his appointed destiny (*Netivot Shalom, Vayeishev*, p. 275). All the components of his dream later did come true. At first all the brothers were together, as symbolized by their binding sheaves together in the field. Joseph's sheaf rising up was fulfilled when he became the ruler of Egypt. The brothers' bowing down was fulfilled when they came down to Egypt for food and prostrated themselves before Joseph, without knowing at that point who he was.

6. In Joseph's second dream, which he related to his father as well as his brothers, he saw the sun, the moon, and eleven stars bowing down to him (Genesis 37:9). Jacob interpreted the sun as representing himself, the moon as representing Rachel, and the stars as representing his other eleven sons. He rejected the dream due to the fact that Rachel was already dead. From this the Sages learn that every dream has some extraneous, nonsensible matter, and that no dream is entirely fulfilled (*Berachot* 55a). Rashi explains that the moon represented Bilhah, who raised Joseph like a son after the death of Rachel.

   Despite Jacob's reprimanding Joseph, the very next verse states: "And his brothers were jealous of him, but his father guarded the matter" (Genesis 37:10). Rashi comments: "He (Jacob) waited and anticipated when it [the dream] would occur." Jacob knew from his own experience that these dreams were not merely figments of Joseph's desire for power but were prophetic in nature. He waited to see when and how they would be fulfilled. Based on the fact that twenty-two years later Joseph's brothers did in fact bow down to him, the Sages state that a person may hope for twenty-two years for the fulfillment of his dreams (*Berachot* 55a–b).

7–8. While in prison in Egypt, Joseph correctly interpreted two dreams for Pharaoh's baker and his cupbearer (Genesis 40:1–23). It could be said that the very concept of psychotherapy can be learned from the following description: "Joseph came to them in the morning and he saw them and behold they were disturbed and he asked.... 'Why are you downcast today?' And they said to him, 'We dreamt a dream and there is no interpreter for it.' And Joseph said to them, 'Do not interpretations belong to God? Please relate it to me' " (Genesis 40:7–8).

   We see from this exchange that dreams have a powerful

influence on people and can affect people's moods in a profound way. Joseph encouraged the two men to discuss their dreams as a way of healing their mental anguish, and he expressed confidence that the dreams could be satisfactorily interpreted. These rather simple ideas form the basis of psychoanalysis in general, as well as the basis for the specific use of dreams in contacting the more unconscious realms of the human psyche. Joseph exemplifies the trust and the empathetic relationship which must exist between any person seeking psychological guidance and a mental health professional. He was able to take the various details of the cupbearer and baker's dreams and construct the main thrust of their messages. This too is the job of the psychologist, as he or she attempts to understand the root causes of the problem from many different pieces of information.

The concept that a dream manifests itself according to its interpretation is learned from what the cupbearer said to Pharaoh when he related Joseph's skill in interpreting dreams: "…and he interpreted for us our dreams; he interpreted for each in accordance with his dream. And it was that just as he interpreted it for us, so did it happen…" (Genesis 41:12–13). This idea is fundamental in the Talmudic discussion of dreams and will be developed more fully later in this chapter.

9–10. The last two dreams in Genesis are those of Pharaoh, which Joseph interpreted and in so doing rose to be the de facto ruler of Egypt. Pharaoh's two dreams were very similar. In his first dream he saw seven healthy cows emerge from the Nile and graze, and then seven ugly and skinny cows emerged from the Nile and consumed the seven healthy ones. His second dream was of seven healthy ears of grain sprouting on one stalk of wheat, followed by the sprouting of seven thin and pitiful ears that were scorched by an eastern wind. The thin ones then consumed the healthy ones (Genesis 41:1–7).

Upon awaking, Pharaoh called his advisors, but none

could interpret the dream. Rashi states that there were in fact interpretations, but Pharaoh did not like them. It is explained that along with the dream Pharaoh was also given its meaning, but he forgot it. When he heard Joseph's interpretation it rang true to him, for deep within he knew that it was the correct interpretation. This can happen to us, too — many times the meanings of our dreams are quite obvious to us, while other times we know the meanings of our dreams intuitively when they are properly interpreted.

In both dreams of Pharaoh, as well as in the dreams of the cupbearer and the baker, Joseph interpreted numbers of objects as representing segments of time. This understanding was crucial to his ability to interpret the dreams. The intrinsic connection of time and space, one of the most important revelations of Albert Einstein, was already perceived by Joseph.

Chassidut teaches that everything in Torah is an allusion to how to best serve God and how to bring out the best within us. The Slonimer Rebbe explains that the seven good cows and seven good ears of grain represent our good characteristics, while the thin cows and ears represent our evil inclination. We must always be on guard lest all our good works and intentions be consumed by our baser desires. He continues to explain that the cows symbolize our carnal desires, while the grain represents our desire for eating. These are the two main drives in man and have the power to consume the Divine soul when not properly subdued. Joseph symbolizes the ability to overcome and transmute these desires for the good. It was he who overcame the advances of the wife of Potiphar, and his wise advice on how to save grain during the years of plenty so there would be what to eat in the years of famine represents his ability to control the forces that fuel the desire to eat (*Netivot Shalom*, *Mikeitz*, p. 268).

It is interesting to note that although each calendar year is different, almost all the ten dreams are read in the yearly Torah cycle during one month, the month of Kislev, which falls out near the winter solstice, the longest nights of the year. The *Sefer Yetzirah*, one of the most ancient of all Kabbalistic texts, assigns a "sense" to each of the months. The five bodily senses are joined by seven others. The "sense" of the month of Kislev is sleep. This is explained to mean the sense of dreaming. Although we all dream, not everyone has a "sense" of dreaming. In the very month where the sense of dreaming is dominant, we read most of the dreams of the five books of Moses.

Along with the ten dreams of Genesis, there are two other cardinal events that occur involving a state of deep sleep — when God separated a side of Adam in order to form woman (Genesis 2:21) and when God forged a covenant with Abraham (Genesis 15:9–21).

Before God separated woman from man, Adam, according to tradition, was an androgynous being. The psychological view that both man and woman have, along with their primary male or female consciousness, the opposite consciousness as well, is rooted in understanding that man and woman were once united in one body and one consciousness. The formation of separate male and female entities occurred on the physical plane, yet all of us at our source still maintain a certain mixture of both states of mind. The deep sleep state of Adam during the process of separating Eve can be understood as not only a sort of anesthesia, but as a metaphor for this primordial act taking place in the deepest levels of the human unconscious, the same source of dream states. The emphasis in the Kabbalah of the unity of masculine and feminine is based on a profound awareness of the unity from which we all trace our primordial source.

The first covenant God made with Abraham, even before circumcision, was the covenant with the land: "On that day God made a covenant with Abram saying, 'To your descendants have I given this land...' " (Genesis 15:18). Preceding this statement God revealed the future of the Jewish people to Abraham in an unconscious state: "And it happened as the sun was setting a deep sleep fell upon Abram; and behold an awesome great darkness fell upon him" (Genesis 15:12). The revelation and the covenant occurring in a deep sleep state represents the almost supernatural existence of the Jewish people and the unique relationship between the Jewish people and God, and the Jewish people and the Land of Israel. Even a superficial overview of history shows that there is no historical precedent for the miraculous survival of the Jewish people and their unbreakable attachment to the Land of Israel. Similar to a dream which transcends normative logic, so too Jewish history transcends all precedent and reason.

# Dreams in the Prophets and the Writings

Regarding the special nature of the prophecy of Moses, God says: "If there should be prophets amongst you, in a vision shall I, God, make Myself known to him; in a dream shall I speak with him. Not so my servant Moses, in all My house he is the trusted one. Mouth to mouth I speak to him, in a clear vision and not in riddles; at the image of God he gazes" (Numbers 12:6–8).

Moses saw God through a "clear lens," while all other prophets received their prophecy through a "cloudy lens" of visions, dreams, or trances. This is not to denegrate the status of other prophets. A person had to be on an extremely high spiritual level to receive true prophecy. God would grant Divine messages and revelations of future events to the prophets of Israel through visions that were full of symbolic language and allusion. The prophet then had to interpret the vision, similar to the interpretation of a dream.

The words of the prophets that are recorded in the Bible are highly symbolic in nature and filled with eternal allegory and import. This symbolic language is very close to the symbolic language of the unconscious speaking to us through our dreams. Only Moses had integrated his subconscious and conscious so totally that he could receive clear prophecy.

Throughout the books of the Prophets and the Writings, dreams are used in two different contexts. The first is as a means of ridiculing false prophets and leaders who misled the people with deceiving dreams. These false prophets were either those who merited lofty levels of consciousness but did not interpret what they received properly, or those who faked it entirely. Here are a few examples of this usage of the word *dream*.

> I have heard what is said by the prophets, who prophesy falsely in My name, saying: "I *have dreamed*, I *have dreamed*." How long [will this be]? Is anything in the heart of the prophets who lie, the prophets of their heart's deceit who think to make My people forget My name *through their dreams*?
>
> (Jeremiah 23:25–27)

> For the oracles have spoken vanity, the diviners have seen false-hood, and the *dreamers* speak lies; they comfort with meaningless words.
>
> (Zechariah 10:2)

> For the exultation of the wicked is recent and the joy of the hypo-crite last but a moment.... He shall fly away *like a dream* and shall not be found; he will be chased away like a vision of the night.
>
> (Job 20:5–8)

Alternatively, the term *dream* is also used to denote a lofty state of consciousness, often connected to revelation and redemption. A few examples:

> And afterwards I shall pour out My spirit on all flesh, and your sons and daughters will prophesize, your old men shall *dream dreams*, and your young men shall see visions....
>
> (Joel 3:1)

> A Song of Ascents: When God will return the captivity of Zion, we will be as *dreamers*.
>
> (Psalms 126:1–2)

This verse begins the psalm recited before Grace after Meals on Shabbat, holidays, and other joyous occasions. The Malbim comments that we will merit to be called dreamers because the Jewish people never gave up its dream to be redeemed, a promise received and handed down by the prophets who received their prophecy in dreams and visions.

The two opposite contexts in which the concept of dreams appears in Scripture alludes to a much deeper understanding of the very nature of dreams, a point to be explained later in this book in chapter 3, "The Paradoxical Nature of Dreams."

Just as in the Pentateuch, dreams play a major role in a number of incidents in the Prophets and the Writings. For example, the book of Judges recounts how the night before a major battle between Midian and Israel, God commands the judge Gideon to disguise himself and go down to the enemy camp. As Gideon enters the camp he hears a man relating a dream to his friend: "Behold I dreamed that a slice of bread was rolling through the camp of Midian and it came to a tent and struck it so that it fell and overturned it...." The other man answered, "This is nothing but the sword of Gideon...for into his hand has God delivered Midian...." Hearing this, Gideon bowed down to the ground and returned to the camp of Israel, where he told the people, "Arise, for God has delivered into your hand the Midianite camp" (Judges 7:13–15).

In the book of Kings, we read about King Solomon, who was but twelve years old when he ascended to the throne. God appeared to him in a dream and told him to make a request and it would be granted. Rather than asking for riches or honor, Solomon asks for wisdom and discernment in judging God's people. God lauds Solomon's good judgment and grants him not only wisdom, but riches and honor as well (Kings I 3:5–15).

The book of Daniel, one of the most enigmatic and mysterious of the books of the Bible, is a string of visions, miracles, and prophecies. Similar to Joseph, who rose to power by interpreting Pharaoh's dreams, Daniel rose to power by interpreting a dream of Nebuchadnezzar. As in many other places in the Bible, it is difficult to discern the fine line between dream, prophecy, and vision in the book of Daniel.

True to God's promise in the book of Numbers, the word of God was received throughout the ages in dreams and visions. Throughout our history it has inspired us as individuals and as a people to strive for lofty heights and to hold out for the promised redemption when we will be, as the psalmist wrote, truly "as dreamers."

# Dreams in the Talmud

The Talmud, which was redacted approximately 1,500 years ago, serves as the main repository of the oral Torah. Encyclopedic in size, it contains a wide-ranging record of the discussions that form the development of Jewish law, ethics, philosophy, and custom. Dreams are mentioned scores of times in many different contexts in the Talmud. The Tractate *Berachot*, in fact, devotes three pages exclusively to this subject. We will concentrate mostly on the various statements and lessons recounted in these pages.

It is crucial to point out that one of the Talmud's goals is to teach one to see truth from many different angles. Even if an opinion is rejected in discussions of Jewish law, the Talmud nonetheless preserves the opinion in order to teach us that although the Sages chose one view over another, there is still a point of truth in the rejected view. The same holds true for discussions of ideas and concepts related to Jewish ethics and philosophy. "These and these are the words of the living God" (*Eruvin* 13a) is the Talmudic dictum expressing this broad concept of truth and reality. The many different and sometimes contradictory statements made by the Sages regarding the nature and meaning of dreams should be viewed in this context. Each idea contains a kernel of truth and should not be seen as exclusive in nature.

Although we cannot, in a book as short as this one, delve extensively into the connection between Jewish sources relating to dreams and modern psychoanalytical theories, it should be noted that many, if not most modern opinions, can be seen quite clearly in the various dreams recorded in the written Torah and the many opinions offered in the oral Torah.

We now present some of the key opinions about dreams (not necessarily in chronological order). In later chapters we will attempt to develop a connection between these various opinions in order to understand the underlying dynamics of dreams.

- "Rav Chisda said: [Let one dream] any dream but a dream of fasting" (Berachot 55a).

  There are a number of opinions by later commentaries regarding what Rav Chisda intended by this statement. One opinion, which can be understood in the words of Rashi, is that to dream of oneself fasting is a negative omen. Another opinion, that of the Aruch (Rabbi Nathan of Rome), is that every dream has some significance other than a dream while fasting, as the lack of food can cause disturbing dreams. This point can be extended to the idea that a wide variety of conditions that affect the body may be the cause of disturbing dreams. The Shaar HaTziyun (220:1) extends this idea even further by stating that anyone who experiences disturbing events during the day should not worry about ominous dreams at night.

- "Rav Chisda said: A negative dream is better than a positive dream" (Berachot 55a).

  Rashi explains that this is because a negative dream will motivate the dreamer to repent and change his or her ways. This is an important point in understanding the potentially healing qualities of dreams.

- "Rav Chisda said: A positive dream is not fulfilled in its entirety, nor is a negative dream fulfilled in its entirety" (Berachot 55a).

  In other words, even a dream that is fulfilled has some extraneous, nonsensical elements. This idea is augmented by a verse from Jeremiah: "The prophet with a dream tells a dream, but one with My word speaks My word of truth. How can the chaff compare to the wheat?" (Jeremiah 23:28). Rabbi Yochanan explains, in the name of Rabbi Shimon ben Yochai, that just as it is impossible to have wheat without some chaff mixed in it, so too it is impossible to have a dream without some senseless matter mixed in it. As mentioned above, Joseph's dream of the sun, moon, and stars is brought as a proof to this idea (Berachot 55a).

- "Rav Chisda further said: A dream that has not been interpreted is like a letter that has not been read" (Berachot 55a).

  Rashi explains this to mean that dreams are in themselves neutral — their meaning and importance is determined by their interpretation. This idea is analyzed by the Talmud at length and becomes one of the cardinal Talmudic principles on dreams. As mentioned above, the verse concerning Joseph's interpretation of the baker and cupbearer's dreams can be understood as teaching that a dream goes after its interpretation. The Talmud relates many stories that confirm this phenomenon. One of these stories is of Rabbi Bana'ah, who went to twenty-four dream interpreters. Each interpreter gave him a different interpretation, yet each and every interpretation was realized! Included in the above stories are those of Sages who were able to accurately interpret dreams and also reveal to the dreamer different sins in his past.

- "Rava said: A dream only follows its interpretation if the interpretation is consistent with the elements in the dream" (Berachot 55b).

- "When Shmuel would see a negative dream he would recite the following verse: 'Dreams speak lies' (Zechariah 10:2). Yet when he would have a good dream he would quote the same verse [in a slightly different manner]: '[But do] dreams speak lies?' " (Berachot 55b).

- Rava raised a difficulty between two seemingly contradictory verses we have quoted (Berachot 55b). One states that God will speak to His prophets through dreams (Numbers 12:7). The other states that dreams tell lies (Zechariah 10:2). Rava answers his own question by saying that it is not really a contradiction: The first case is when the dream is sent through the agency of an angel, the second case is when it is through the agency of a demon.

- Although the Talmud brings many stories and opinions confirming the prophetic nature of dreams, and we have already seen the prophetic nature of the ten dreams of Genesis, Rabbi Shmuel bar Nachmani questions the entire concept of dreams being prophetic by stating that a dream is nothing more than a product of the dreamer's own thoughts (*Berachot* 55b). Two stories are brought to show this point. A king and a caesar in separate incidents ask a sage to tell them what they would dream that evening. In both stories the sage described a dream, and sure enough each dreamt the dream he was told about. We will later see how this opinion does not necessarily conflict with the prophetic nature of dreams.

Along with the above discussions, the Talmud gives a long and fascinating appraisal of the significance of seeing different objects, people, places, words, and actions in a dream. Assigning fixed meanings to the various images and figures of our dream worlds, interestingly enough, was taken up by Western psychoanalysis in the last hundred years, and it plays a major part in modern dream analysis.

It is worthwhile to mention a few other important teachings about dreams from the Talmud. Rabbi Huna bar Ami taught that if one is distressed about a dream he should have it interpreted by three people. The Talmud asks, if a dream that is not interpreted is like a letter that has not been read, why would one want to have it interpreted? It answers that Rabbi Huna does not mean the dream should be interpreted, but rather that it should be "remedied." The following procedure should be followed: The person who is distressed by his dream should go to three of his friends and declare: "I have seen a good dream." They should say to him: "It is good and may it be good. May the Merciful One transform it for the better. May it be decreed upon you seven times from Heaven that it be good." The listeners then recite three verses of transformation, three of redemption, and three of peace. One should make sure to go to friends for this procedure, for when Joseph told his dreams to his brothers, who were already jealous of him, they hated him even more (*Berachot* 55b).

According to Jewish law, one who has a disturbing dream is allowed to fast even on Shabbat. This teaches us how serious the matter of dreams is taken in Judaism, for Shabbat is a holy day, when fasting is normally prohibited. We are taught that one may only fast on Shabbat if that will bring him peace of mind, which is within the spirit of Shabbat. Some say that today we should not fast on Shabbat, as we no longer have a true tradition of how to interpret dreams. Others say one should only fast if one has had the dream three times (*Shulchan Aruch, Orach Chaim* 220, 226).

Another practice described in the Talmud for one who is distressed by a dream is to recite a beautiful prayer requesting that God heal him and transform the dream to the good. The prayer should be recited while the priests are reciting the priestly blessing (*Berachot* 55b). It is included in most holiday prayer books.

The Bible and the Talmud have many more discussions on dreams, and the reader is encouraged to look them up further in the sources. Torah literature is replete with incredible insights into the nature of dreams, especially as they pertain to the realm of human psychology. We have only brought a small sampling of these insights here in order to help us with our analysis of the nature of dreams and how they relate to modern psychology.

Before we move further in our study we must first understand the concept of symbolism and how it relates to dreams, reality, and Torah.

2

# Understanding Symbolism

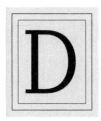reams are the language of the unconscious, the sub-conscious, and the superconscious. By the uncon-scious we mean the strata of unrecognized feelings and motivations hidden deep within the psyche. The subconscious relates as well to hidden emotions and perceptions, but it is just below the surface, ever ready to thrust itself into consciousness. The superconscious relates to the soul in its pristine, Divine form. It is an all-encompassing force in the human psyche, yet it is usually hidden and overwhelmed by normative consciousness.

Dreams are the mechanism by which these more hidden aspects of our psyche communicate, since they filter and react to the vast amount of physical, emotional, and spiritual data bombarding our senses during our waking hours. The human mind and psyche consists of a complex layering of consciousness. Every human being has to deal with reality on many different levels — instinctual, emotional, intellectual, and spir-itual. Each person must juggle a myriad of fears, hopes, and disappoint-ments. Dreams translate the manner in which we experience the world into symbolic language and image. That they communicate to us in such a fantastic, colorful, and baffling way is what makes them so intriguing.

The ability to communicate is considered the very defining quality of humanity. This idea is learned from the verse: "And God formed the man of dust from the ground and He blew into his nostrils the soul of life; and man became a living being" (Genesis 2:7). Onkelos, in his classic Aramaic translation of the Bible, translates "living being" as "a speaking spirit." The ability to communicate beyond what is necessary for survival is what ultimately differentiates man from animal. As the verse indicates, the soul of man and our ability to communicate are intrinsically connected.

Dreams are not the only thing that incorporate and use symbolism as a means of expression. All languages are actually based on symbolism and association. In most ancient languages letters were pictograms, and even today a letter is a symbol for a sound. Every culture attaches certain associations to words, whose rich and subtle meanings are conveyed in the context of that society. This is why idioms do not translate well, or at all, into other languages, as those expressions can only really be understood within the specific associations of that society.

Symbols are used prominently in virtually every aspect of our lives. Their practical and spiritual effect can be seen in religion, commerce, media, mathematics, science, art, and more. Symbols conjure up deep and powerful associations, communicating love or hate, fear or hope, belonging or exclusion.

Even the way we experience reality is "dreamlike" in nature, usually, though not always, far less dramatic than the theatrical progression of dreams. Each person relates to reality in his or her own way, creating a personal, symbolic lens through which to process life. A multitude of people can experience the same event at the same time, yet each one draws a different conclusion and sees the situation through his own personal associations and history.

All levels of a person's consciousness are connected by the symbols he or she chooses to invest with meaning and power. Experiences during waking reality and sleep states are intrinsically meshed together, and in fact many people actually spend a good part of their waking hours dreaming as well. The more we realize the complexity of the human psyche, the more in touch we can be with all the different aspects of our being.

# Symbolism and Torah

We are taught in the *Zohar*: "God looked into the Torah and created the world" (*Zohar* 2:16). The Torah is the blueprint from which all physical and spiritual worlds were constructed. As a result, symbolism is integral to the Torah. The very essence of Torah is multifaceted and open to a myriad of interpretations and perspectives.

Torah, as the manifest will of an infinite God, is essentially infinite in its depths of meaning. The soul of man, which is essentially a "part of God above," as taught in Chassidic thought, likewise shares this infinite aspect in potential. Just as each person relates to reality in his or her own way and in so doing creates his or her own dream world, similarly each person relates to and understands Torah from his or her own unique perspective.

It is stated in the *Zohar* that there are seventy faces to the Torah (*Zohar* 1:47b), similar to a prism that changes color and light with every slight turn. Rabbi Yitzchak Luria, known as the Arizal, the great Kabbalist of Safed, posits that there are 600,000 faces to the Torah, one for each soul root in Israel. Both of these teachings attempt to convey the same message regarding the very nature of the Torah and of reality. (Interestingly, the teachings of quantum physics also recognize the impossibility of establishing one "objective" reality and explain that consciousness affects reality in such a way that it is virtually impossible to quantify and is therefore ever changing.)

One system of Jewish learning which is built upon the idea of multiple layers of interpretation is called "*Pardes*," an acronym for four levels of understanding text: *peshat* — the simple, literal meaning; *remez* — the meaning that is alluded to or hinted at; *derash* — the allegorical, metaphorical meaning; and *sod* — the mystical, secret meaning.

Each word and verse, each story and commandment in the Torah contains all four of these basic levels. Symbolism plays an important part in the realms of *derash* and *sod*, both of which help us to understand the relevance of the text for each person in every generation. The stories in the Torah are not just one-time events that happened to individuals a long time ago, but rather are archetypal in nature and represent various physical and spiritual energies that are ever present in each and every person and in all aspects of reality. This point is crucial to understanding the essence of Torah and is the quintessential understanding of symbolism — that a symbol captures a plethora of meaning, much greater than the outside, finite form indicates. In the words of the Midrash, they are "the little that holds much" (*Bereishit Rabbah* 9:7).

The stories of the Torah are therefore true on many levels simultaneously. Through the simple narrative of actual occurrences, the Torah gives over multilayers of symbolism, allegory, and metaphor. The story of Adam and Eve in the Garden of Eden, for example, along with its deep revelation of the primordial beginnings of mankind, serves as a profound allegory for the basic existential reality of humanity. As eplained by the oral Torah, Kabbalah, and Chassidut, the story teaches profound lessons on human relationships; desire, inner conflict, and temptation; the interaction of mind, soul, and body; objective and subjective knowledge; and the nature of choice and its consequences.

Similarly, the story of Jacob and Esau represents the battle between physical and material, body and soul. Amalek, who attacked the weak and the stragglers of the Jewish people as they wandered in the desert, symbolizes evil. Korach, who challenged Moses for leadership, is the symbol of corruption by power. The dynamics of sibling rivalry are revealed in the stories of Cain and Abel and Joseph and his brothers. The exile and redemption of the Jewish people in Egypt embodies the essential secret of cycles as they manifest in the human body, in the emotional and psychological realms, in nature and the seasons, and in Jewish and world history.

The Torah's description of Creation, transmitted in sweeping generalities and symbolism, sheds great light on the Divine creative process and its meaning to man, who is made in the image of God. (As an aside, it is noteworthy that recent discoveries in physics and cosmology confirm in great measure the wisdom revealed in the Torah account of Creation. What were once thought to be two conflicting versions of events are now being seen more and more as two languages describing the same event.) Through seemingly simple narratives, the Bible reveals the very depths of human psychology and the existential condition of man.

Carl Jung, one of the fathers of modern psychology, recognized the power of symbols and created an entire language to describe the archetypal imagery of dreams. Although his language was new, the idea of archetypal figures and symbolic association has been deeply rooted in Jewish thought for millennium.

# Symbolism and the Hebrew Letters

At the very core of Torah symbolism are the Hebrew letters, the basic building blocks of creation. Each letter is a channel of Divine flow into the world, a concentrated packet of energy manifesting itself in all realms of the physical word and at all levels of human consciousness. Kabbalists view the Hebrew letters as the building blocks of the world, just like a scientist views atoms and molecules.

According to Jewish thought, God created the world from speech and continues to create through the use of the Hebrew letters. As such, the form, name, and numerical equivalent of each letter contain profound insight and reveal wisdom from the practical to the mystical. A word in Hebrew is not just a combination of sounds but is actually the spiritual force animating and giving life to that which it describes. The name is thus the actual essence of the person or entity.

In order to understand these ideas more deeply, let us consider what we can learn from the letters which compose the Hebrew word for "dream," חלום.

The form of the letter *chet*, ח, according to the Arizal, resembles a gateway through which one enters and exits. The *chet* consists of a *vav* (ו), the symbol of the masculine, and a *zayin* (ז), the symbol of the feminine, connected by a thin pyramid-shaped bridge. This form symbolizes a groom and bride standing under a wedding canopy, a *chuppah*, which begins with the letter *chet*. Groom and bride enter the gateway of the canopy single, yet leave married. Dreams emanate in part from a deep level of the superconscious where an impression of the united being of Adam and Eve, before their separation, still exists. Dreams touch the place within where the masculine and feminine principle struggle for their proper and balanced expression.

The image of the gateway applies in general to entering higher levels of experience or consciousness and then returning renewed and revitalized. We see it, for example, in the weekly cycle of six weekdays concluding with Shabbat, which serves as both the culmination of the previous week and the source of all blessing for the coming week. The *vav* of the letter *chet* equals six, representing the six days of work, and the *zayin* equals seven, representing the seventh day, Shabbat. The connecting bridge is the transition between these two experiences of time and reality. In relation to the week, Shabbat is like a "dream," a peaceful utopia and an almost out-of-this-world experience.

Another example of this phenomenon of bridging different states of consciousness is, of course, dreaming, in that we enter our unconscious, subconscious, and superconscious worlds every time we sleep. The Talmud teaches that sleep is one-sixtieth of death (*Berachot* 57b). The first thing a Jew does upon awakening in the morning is recite the "*Modeh Ani*" prayer, voicing his or her appreciation to God for returning his soul and granting him another day. As we have seen from the Biblical overview above, dreams are also a gateway to a superconscious state where an individual may receive Divine messages, insight, and direction. The key is to translate and integrate those dream experiences into our lives. The "sense" of dreaming we mentioned above, relating to the month of Kislev, is the ability to bridge the conscious and unconscious parts of our lives and use our dream states constructively.

The letter *chet* is closely related to the word *chiyut*, which means "life force." Experiments have revealed that sleep deprivation leads to death. Although it is a mystery of sorts, every human being needs to spend up to a third of his life literally unconscious. This time is not wasted but is actually imperative to life itself.

The numerical value of *chet* is eight. While the number seven represents the idea of complete cycles, the number eight symbolizes eternity and a state above time and space, beyond logic and reason. The covenant of circumcision occurs on the eighth day of the life of a male child. Both the number eight and the concept of covenant symbolize a relationship beyond normative logic. Dreams similarly are experienced as beyond time and space and seem, at least initially, to be beyond reason and logic.

The *lamed*, ל, the second letter in the word *chalom*, is the tallest of all the letters, ascending above the line of the script. The Sages refer to the *lamed* as "a tower soaring in the air" (*Chagigah* 15b). The word *lamed* means to learn and to teach, and in this sense symbolizes the aspiration of man to understand the world he lives in, the desire to reach ever higher levels of soul consciousness, and the passion to ultimately unite with his Creator. Similarly, interpreting a dream is an attempt to understand our dynamic inner world and to comprehend any signs we may be receiving from Above.

*Lamed* is the first letter of the word *lev*, לב, which means "heart." Dreams are primarily experienced in the heart, the symbolic seat of the emotions. The second letter of *lev* is a *beit*, which equals two. Rabbi Avraham Abulafia, a great Kabbalist, states that the word *lev* can thus be understood as "two *lameds*," and when two *lameds* are placed face to face they form the shape of a heart. Rashi explains that when the Torah teaches us to love God "with all your heart" (Deuteronomy 6:5), this refers to both the good and the evil inclinations. Dreams in many instances are a classic battleground between the two inclinations of the heart.

The numerical value of *lamed* is thirty, the number of days of a full month in the Jewish calendar. The experience of dreaming is very connected to the secret of time, as will be explained later in this book. The Jewish calendar is based on the moon, which goes through a cycle of birth, fullness, death, and rebirth each month. Similarly, waking and sleeping also represent a birth/death cycle, as each time we sleep our souls leave our bodies (leading to the Talmudic statement quoted above that sleep is one-sixtieth of death).

The form of the letter *vav,* ו, of *chalom* represents a pillar, or a man standing upright with his feet on the earth and his head reaching the heavens, just like the image of the ladder Jacob saw in his dream. The letter *vav* means "and," as we see from its very first appearance in the Torah, in the very first verse: "In the beginning God created the heavens and the earth." It is the twenty-second letter of the Torah and it begins the word ואת, composed of the first and last letters of the Hebrew alphabet. The power of the *vav* is to connect all the forces of Creation, symbolized by the twenty-two Hebrew letters.

A unique aspect of the letter *vav* is that it is used in the Torah to invert a verb tense from past to future and future to past. This phenomenon gives the Torah an eternal quality, a sense of being both within and yet transcending time. The ability to transform the past is the secret of *teshuvah*, repentance. We are taught that when one returns to God in sincere repentance, motivated by the fear or awe of God, his past deliberate sins become like inadvertent errors. When he returns to God from pure love, his past transgressions actually become merits, as they now motivate him to serve God with added zeal and enthusiasm (*Yoma* 86b).

Just as we have the power to change our past into the future, we also have the ability to draw the future into the present and the past. Through dreaming and visualizing the future, we manifest that energy in the present and even into the past as we change our perspective. The World to Come, a future state of perfected existence, is in fact already manifest in the present for those who are able to connect and draw upon that energy and state of consciousness.

In addition to dreaming at night, the average person is said to spend up to an hour and a half or more a day daydreaming. In other words, we are continually going in and out of various levels of consciousness and living in an amalgamation of past, present, and future. Dreams are the connecting force of both time and consciousness, as we balance having our feet on the ground and our heads in the heavens.

In addition to the *vav* connecting time, it also represents the six planes of a cube, the cardinal symbol of space, since its numerical value is six. The *vav* represents the force that connects space and time in what Einstein called the space-time continuum. This is the secret of God creating the world in six days. The Sages point out that in the first verse of the Torah the letter *alef* appears six times. A*lef* means "one thousand." This serves as the textual support for the tradition that this present cycle of history will last six thousand years, followed by the Messianic era.

Dreams are beyond time and space, yet within their bounds as well. Dreams connect our conscious reality to our unconscious and superconscious. While a man stands on the ground, his dreams lift his head to the heavens, from spiritual world to spiritual world, where he draws down timeless Divine inspiration and insight to enlighten his journey on earth.

The *mem*, מ, the last letter of the word *chalom*, symbolizes life-giving water in all its forms. The Hebrew word for water, מים, consists of an open *mem* and a closed *mem*, with the letter *yud* in between. The *yud* represents a single drop of water, while the open *mem* symbolizes a fountain of flowing water above the ground and the closed, final *mem* symbolizes an underground source of water. Water relates to wisdom, and in particular to the wisdom of Torah. Dreams when properly understood give us great insight and wisdom into our problems and challenges, as well as how to solve them. The dream state is fluid by nature, a river of flowing images and symbols collecting in our mind's eye before it slips away.

The letter *mem* equals forty and symbolizes transition and change throughout the Torah. The flood in the generation of Noah came as a result of rain, which destroyed the world. The Jews wandered in the desert for forty years until a new generation was ready to enter the Land of Israel. Moses spent forty days on Mount Sinai receiving the Torah and another two periods of forty days gaining atonement for the sin of the golden calf and receiving the second tablets of the law. A *mikveh*, the ritual bath of purification, consists of a minimum of forty *se'ah* of water. All these examples represent transition and change. Dreams also represent transition, for they bring hidden desires, fears, and hopes into the open.

The opening to the Temple Hall in Solomon's Temple in Jerusalem was forty cubits high. This relates back to the ability to enter and exit, as symbolized by the *chet*, the first letter of *chalom*. The power of the soul to enter and exit different levels of consciousness and transition between past, present, and future is the mature "sense" of dreaming.

*Mashiach*, the Hebrew word for Messiah, begins with a *mem* and ends with a *chet*, the exact opposite of *chalom*. We dream of a perfected, ideal existence to be revealed at the end of days, when "the knowledge of God will cover the earth like the waters cover the seabed" (Isaiah 11:9). This will take place during the Messianic era, which will herald an age when "your sons and your daughters will prophesy, your old men will dream dreams and your young men will see visions" (Joel 3:1). The waters of knowledge will be healing waters and dreams will be synonymous with continually higher levels of consciousness and divine revelation. Both the *chet* and the *mem* symbolize life. The Messianic era, the fulfillment of the collective dream of the Jewish people, will culminate in the resurrection of the dead, when death will be "swallowed up forever" (Isaiah 25:8) and when past, present, and future will unfold simultaneously.*

The key of symbolism unlocks the door to understanding dreams, while comprehension of divine allegory and metaphor unlocks the doors to understanding Torah. To grasp the secret of life is to view the world with "Torah-colored glasses," seeing through the masks of plurality and symbols, all the while turning our dreams into reality.

---

\* Many of the above insights on the letters are found in or based on ideas in the book *The Hebrew Letters* by Rabbi Yitzchak Ginsburgh (Jerusalem: Gal Einai, 1990).

# 3

# The Paradoxical Nature of Dreams

The various teachings on dreams presented in the Talmud range from relegating dreams to the realm of nonsense or viewing them as mere replays of the day's events, to attributing to them great significance, as indications of prophecy and messages from God. As we pointed out above, these various teachings should not be seen as exclusive, ruling out all other ideas presented; rather, they each contain points of truth which can be pulled together and understood in a broad picture. In this chapter we will examine the paradoxical nature of dreams, and in the following one we will present an integrative and holistic model through which to understand their various manifestations.

In the previous chapter we explained how the individual letters of the word *chalom*, dream, help us understand the essence of dreams. Now we will probe further to understand the root meaning of the word *chalom*. Most words in the Hebrew language have a three-letter root, of which two are the essential letters. In *chalom*, the two essential letters are the *chet* and the *lamed*. We can examine the many meanings of this root to gain insight into its essence.

The letters *chet* and *lamed* are the root of the words "sick," *choleh*; "disease," *machalah*; and "weakness," *chalishut*. Yet the same letters form the root of *chayil*, which means "strength" or "military troops." *Eishet chayil*, which means a "woman of valor," is the song from Proverbs traditionally sung in every household on Shabbat eve. In Aramaic, a language closely associated with Hebrew, the root *chet-lamed* means both "bitter" and "sweet." Paradoxically, not only does the root *chet-lamed* mean sickness, but it is also at the root of the word for becoming healthy, *lehachlim*, a word very close to *lachalom*, "to dream."

The weekdays are called *chol*, again from the root *chet-lamed*. Adding another *lamed* to the end of the root *chet-lamed* yields the word *chilul*, profanity, the strongest form of the root word, or *chalal*, a corpse. Rabbi Yitzchak Ginsburgh explains that in truth sickness is an intermediary state between holiness and life and profanity and death (represented by a corpse). In other words, being sick is in a sense neutral. How we react to the sickness will determine whether the sickness will be a positive or a negative experience. If our sickness alerts us to the dangers of an unhealthy lifestyle or abuse of the body and leads us to make real and substantial changes to our life, then having been sick can be seen retroactively as having been a blessing. However, if we continue to ignore the signs our body is sending us, then sickness can lead to death. Fever, for example, is the way the body burns poisons. Though it is termed sickness, it is actually part of the process of healing.*

These same ideas apply to dreams. Dreams are like formless raw material, termed *chomer gelem* in Hebrew. The first two letters of the root of *chomer* and the second two letters of *gelem* are the letters of *chalom*, dream. How we shape the raw material of a dream will determine whether its effect on us will be positive or negative. A dream can drag us down to the depths of fear and despair or lift us up to the very heavens. The paradoxical nature of dreams is that they contain the roots of both sickness and health, weakness and strength, bitterness and sweetness.

---

* See *Body, Mind, and Soul* by Rabbi Yitzchak Ginsburgh (Jerusalem: Gal Einai, 2004), pp. 127–131.

We can now understand why Rav Chisda said, "A negative dream is better than a positive dream" (*Berachot* 55a). The effect of a negative dream is so much stronger when related to in a proper way. Rav Chisda also stated, "The sadness of a negative dream suffices for it; the joy of a positive dream suffices for it" (*Berachot* 55a). Rashi explains that the sadness the dreamer experiences after a negative dream serves as an atonement, canceling the need for the dream to be fulfilled, "for its sadness suffices for it." Another meaning of the root *chet-lamed* is *mechilah*, pardon, indicating the potential aspect of psychological healing within dreams.

We can now understand the Talmudic statement that a dream is determined by its interpretation — "all dreams follow the mouth" (*Berachot* 55b). Dreams by nature are neutral, even when they initially appear to be either positive or negative. The interpretation of a dream or the way we reframe it has the power to transform even the worse nightmare into something positive. Life is full of instances in which what first appears to be a disaster becomes a hidden blessing, and what first seems to be a blessing turns into quite the opposite. It is interesting to note that the numerical value of *chalom* is 84, and that of *peh*, mouth, is 85. In other words, a dream leads into the interpretation of the mouth!

The teaching that dreams follow the mouth can be linked to two other famous Talmudic dictums. Several pages after its discussion on dreams, the Talmud states that "all that God does, He does for the good" (*Berachot* 60b). This statement is echoed by the phrase coined by Rabbi Nachum, "This [negative event] too is for the good" (*Taanit* 21a). The importance of interpreting not just dreams, but all reality as being "also for the good" is deeply ingrained in Jewish consciousness. Psychologically it answers how the Jewish people were able to survive millennia of exile, pogrom, and insult, yet survive, while maintaining not only their sanity, but a sense of humor as well. Taking responsibility for our lives and our fates is also a philosophy deeply ingrained in the Jewish people. If you have a bad dream, you can turn it to the good.

Another very important idea in Jewish thought is the power of speech. The model of God creating the world from speech is a model not taken lightly. Our speech can destroy, belittle, and embarrass, or it can inspire, encourage, and create, depending on how we use it. Using speech for gossip, slander, or profanity is strictly forbidden in the Torah. On the other hand, a large part of our tradition is transmitted orally, via the oral tradition.

This then is the source of the advice to go to three people, preferably friends, in the advent of a disturbing dream. Their concern and verbal support is part of the psychological dynamic that turns a dream into the good. "All of Israel is responsible one for the other" (*Shevuot* 39a), and the power of love and friendship can help sweeten any bitterness.

The Maharsha, author of a deeply insightful commentary on the Talmud, offers the following explanation to the various seeming contradictions in the three pages of *Berachot* we analyzed above: There are three types of dreams, he says. The first type of dream is one with no particular meaning, which is open to many different interpretations. This dream is like an unread letter. Giving an affirming spin to this sort of dream strengthens the positive aspects of the dream and in so doing gives it an energy that can then be transformed into reality.

A second type of dream does have a certain prophetic direction or message to the dreamer, but even these dreams can be turned to the good through repentance, i.e., heeding the message and drawing the proper conclusions. As we recite in our prayers on Rosh HaShanah and Yom Kippur: "Repentance, prayer, and charity remove an evil decree."

The third type of dream has true prophetic meaning and is destined to come true. This, for example, is the type of dream Rava said comes from an angel. Many of the Biblical dreams fall into this category, and they are fulfillments of God's promise that in a vision or a dream He would speak to His prophets.

The Sages who stated that dreams are not prophetic were referring to the first type of dream, which is open to many different possibilities and conclusions. A positive interpretation will therefore help determine its basic energy and how it manifests itself. It is also this sort of dream that may be total nonsense, or the result of fasting or other physical or mental disturbances. Rava calls these dreams those that come through the agency of a "demon," which can be understood to be a negative or unbalanced inner psychic force.

Knowing which type of dream we are dealing with is perhaps the key to understanding a dream. For this knowledge one needs to pray for true Divine guidance.

# The Art of Clarification

The ability to identify the source of one's thoughts, feelings, and behavior depends on what is called in Chassidut the art of clarification, which is intrinsically connected to the faculty of imagination. The dreams we dream each night are very connected to our subconscious and, as discussed in the Talmud, follow in many cases what we fill our minds with during our waking hours. Our dreams are mirror images of our own consciousness and our rectified or distorted sense of imagination. Understanding the paradoxical dialectic of dreams requires insight into the very roots of human consciousness.

We discussed above briefly the archetypal nature of the story of Adam and Eve in the Garden of Eden. The name *Adam* can be separated into two syllables: A-*dam*. *Dam* means blood and symbolizes the body, the earthly, material component of man, whereas the letter *alef*, the A, represents the soul, the Godly aspect of man. We learn from this that a human being at his very essence is composed of two opposite energies.

This bipolar dynamic is further symbolized in the Divine directive not to eat from the Tree of Knowledge of Good and Evil. This tree symbolizes the fractured consciousness which is born of losing sight of the unity of all things. Adam and Eve eating of the tree represents a "fall" in consciousness from a unified vision of reality to a more dualistic perception of life; from experiencing good and evil outside of themselves to a reality where good and evil had become internalized. These two forces manifest within us as the *yetzer hatov* and *yetzer hara*, the good and evil inclinations.

The purpose of Torah and mitzvot is to assist us in bridging this dualistic reality while we learn to unite soul and body and all other apparent opposites. This initial dualistic existential reality is the source of man's consciousness and it fuels our dream world, both when awake and when asleep. Yet deep inside each person's superconsciousnes is a distant memory, an impression deep in the soul, of a time in the primordial past when our being and our perception of reality was one of unity.

The struggle for control of the mind is an ongoing battle. We are bombarded daily with an overwhelming amount of stimuli from the outside world, as well as a volcano of conflicting inner feelings, each vying for our attention. The Baal Shem Tov taught that a person is where his thoughts are, and we all know how far away we can be in our minds, while our bodies remain quite stationary.

The mitzvah of not straying after our eyes and after our hearts (Numbers 15:39) is one of the six constant mitzvot which apply to every Jew, at every moment. It is also one of the hardest to fulfill, for the mind is like a wild stallion who pushes away anyone trying to train it. Yet the mind can be trained to a great degree. We can choose between an untrained, wild imagination that drags us after it, or a rectified imagination, which becomes a vessel for Divine inspiration and prophecy. Like dreams, imagination is neither positive nor negative in essence; rather, its raw power can go in either direction.

The Hebrew word for imagination is *dimyon*, from the root *dam*, blood, the same root which appears in A*dam*, man. The power of imagination and fantasy can drag us after our very physical, animal natures, or it can be harnessed to reveal the deepest creative power of the soul. Dreams are intimately connected to the faculty of imagination, and both reflect images of our deep-seated conscious and unconscious powers and inner conflicts.

We learned above that the letter *lamed* is the first letter of the word *lev*, whose two letters can be read "two *lameds*," implying two sides of the heart. The mitzvah to love God with "all your heart," which Rashi explains as loving God with both the good and the evil inclination, serves as a model for everything we do. Our goal is not to obliterate our evil inclination, but rather to train it to serve our higher souls and ultimately God. Once, the Sages attempted to wipe out sexual desire from the world. When they saw that there were no more eggs being produced, they realized that even physical desire has its place and its hour (*Yoma* 69b).

The figure in the Bible who most represents the ability to not just conquer but also direct these inner forces in a positive manner is Joseph. His ability to fend off the continual advances of the wife of Potiphar earned him the name "Joseph the Tzaddik" — Joseph the Righteous. Jewish tradition has long recognized the sexual drive in man as one of the most powerful and primary forces at all levels of consciousness. From the snake in the Garden of Eden, to the story of Joseph in Genesis, to scores of teachings and stories in the Midrash, Talmud, Kabbalah, and Chassidut, we continually see evidence of this powerful force within the body and psyche of man. Joseph took this force, which is very connected to the power of imagination, and transformed it into the keen ability to clarify the symbols of dreams, also very connected to the power of imagination.

The Talmud states that Joseph knew seventy languages (*Sotah* 36b). His knowledge of the inherent symbolism in language is very connected to his skill in interpreting and clarifying dreams. The Hebrew word for interpreting dreams used throughout the story of Joseph is *patar*, פתר. Rabbi Yitzchak Ginsburgh teaches that the same letters arranged differently spell *tofer*, תפר, meaning "to sew." Joseph was able to take diverse symbols in a dream and rearrange them, and then to sew them together to create a unified interpretation. When Jacob blessed Joseph at the end of his life, he began the blessing with the words, "Joseph is a fruitful bough, a fruitful bough by a well, whose branches run over the wall" (Genesis 49:22). The word for "fruitful" is *porat*, פרת, which has the same letters as the words for "to interpret" and "to sew."

The connection between the symbols of language and the symbols of dreams is found in the discussion in the Talmud preceding the three pages in Tractate B*erachot* devoted to dreams. Rav Yehudah states that Bezalel, the chief artisan appointed to construct the Tabernacle in the desert, knew how to join the letters with which heaven and earth were created. God "filled him with a Godly spirit; with wisdom, with understanding, and with knowledge" (Exodus 35:31). The same attributes are mentioned regarding the Creation of the world: "God founded the earth with wisdom, He established the heavens with understanding; through His knowledge the depths were cleaved" (Proverbs 3:19–20). The Tabernacle is considered the microcosm of the Creation. Bezalel was able to construct it by arranging the letters of the holy language through which the heavens and earth were created.

We can learn from Bezalel's method of arranging the letters to create the Tabernacle how to arrange the symbols of a dream in order to interpret dreams. Each detail in a dream is significant and highly symbolic, yet many dreams at first seem disjointed and lacking a coherent meaning and purpose. The art of clarification, which only comes from a rectified consciousness, aids us in seeing beyond the superficial in order to arrive at the essence of each symbol, to relate it to the one dreaming, and then to arrange them all into a cohesive whole, revealing the inner light and purpose of the dream.

*Tardemah*, the deep state of sleep mentioned in the stories of Adam and Abraham, also has the root of *dam*, blood. The numerical value of *tardemah* is 649, the same as *targum*, which means "to translate." To interpret and to translate are obviously connected. The letter *reish*, ר, of both these words means "head," the seat of imagination and consciousness and the place where the art of clarification, *birrur* (which has two *reish*es), occurs.

The letter *reish* equals two hundred, which is the numerical value of the word *kadmon*, which means "primordial." For the art of clarification to succeed it must delve into the most primordial aspects of consciousness where man's deepest energies lie. Deep within man are both animal and Divine souls, and only by confronting and conquering his deepest fears and insecurities can man free himself to fulfill his or her greatest potential.

As our inclinations can be trained and directed, so too, in certain aspects, can our dreams. "Think good and it will be good" is a simple yet potent Chassidic formula for a happy life. The existential reality of man is highly paradoxical and so is the world we live in. God is called the One who "sustains opposites" (*Likkutei Torah* 3:68a). The world He has created, and mankind which He made in His image, reflect this reality and ultimately have the ability to sustain opposites as well.

4

# The Ladder of Dreams

henever there are a number of contradictory ideas regarding a particular subject, it is important and helpful to create an integrated model of the ideas in order to reveal their inner consistency and logic. We have discussed a number of times the importance of seeing various statements recorded in the Talmud, and the Torah in general, as being complementary and not as mutually exclusive. Therefore, we will propose a five-rung ladder which will serve as a model for the various contradictory ideas presented above in relation to dreams. This ladder, which will be seen to correspond to the five names of the soul, also, appropriately enough, brings to mind the ladder in Jacob's dream.

The five names of the soul, as learned from an ancient *midrash*, are *nefesh, ruach, neshamah, chayah,* and *yechidah* (Bereishit Rabbah 14:9). Each name refers to an ascending hierarchy of soul powers and serves as a powerful tool in analyzing and understanding the human psyche.

*Nefesh*, the lowest level of the soul, refers to what is commonly termed "the animal soul," the instinctual and behaviorist drives and patterns of human action associated with man's body. *Ruach*, or "spirit," relates to the emotions; *neshamah*, the inner soul, is considered the seat of the intellect; *chayah*, "the living one," refers to the interaction be-

tween the consciousness and its superconscious origin; and *yechidah*, "the single, unique one," relates to the most Divine aspect of soul. These five levels of soul serve as a beautiful paradigm for understanding the origins of different types of dreams.

The first type of dream can be seen to emanate from the lower soul, the *nefesh*. The example given above is "any dream but a dream of fasting." This type of dream may be the product of the body's craving for food. In other words, the lack of food produces in the body sensations that give birth to the images in a dream. Other bodily needs often influence the nature of dreams.

Sigmund Freud, the famous early-twentieth-century psychologist, put great emphasis on the sexual nature and symbolism of all dreams and the lasting effects of child fantasies and complexes throughout adult life. Although Freud discovered a certain level of truth regarding dream symbolism and the human psyche, his views on dreams and the spiritual component of man were narrow and incomplete. His greatest student, Carl Jung, who believed strongly in the more spiritual aspects of the soul and their influence on dreams, broke away from Freud in order to develop a much fuller and holistic view of the origin and spiritual purpose of dreams.

Corresponding to the *ruach*, the emotional makeup of the psyche, are dreams that tend to replay recent life events or fragments of one's thoughts during the day. Just beneath the surface of the waking conscious self is the subconscious. Dreams of daily events that are filtered and experienced by the subconscious tend to give us quite a different perspective on life. Through dreams, the subconscious reveals the raw emotions bubbling below the surface of the more controlled reactions of the public self. Repressed reactions to daily events such as anger, fear, insecurity, and jealousy tend to come out in dreams that are fueled by the emotions.

Although the intellect is an independent power in the soul, it is nonetheless very much connected to the emotional side of man. Dreams at the level of the *neshamah*, the intellect, are similar in certain aspects to the preceding level in that they too are produced by the events and figures of real life situations, but the difference is that here the intellect is working to find solutions and rectification. At the level of the emotions, dreams are produced by feelings; at the level of intellect dreams are trying to work through the feelings in order to reach a resolution of the problem

It is at the level of the conscious *neshamah* that the idea of a dream going after the interpretation is most potent, for once awake the intellect can take the impressions of a dream, even if quite negative, and reframe it to be good. Alternatively, through the force of will the intellect can decide to make the proper changes in behavior so that a negative dream will serve as the motivation for positive change.

Another example of a dream of the *neshamah* is the teaching that one who toils in Torah during the day can receive innovative Torah ideas in his or her dreams. This type of dream is not just a creative replay of the day's events, but the work of the intellect, which is still active even while we are asleep. Similar to how the subconscious is active, albeit under the surface, during the waking hours, so too, the conscious intellect continues to act below the surface of the subconscious during a dream state.

Other practices are connected to this level of soul and dreaming as well. Modern dream researchers teach various ways of directing and remembering dreams. Suggestions include consciously directing the mind before going to sleep to dream and to subsequently remember the dream or dreams. Upon awaking it is recommended to direct the mind to remember one's dreams immediately and if possible to write them down. A full fifty percent of a dream's content escapes the memory within five minutes of waking and ninety percent within but ten minutes. However, there are different mental training exercises which can help a person become an active participant in his or her dreams in order to confront fears and obstacles at their source and banish them.

These practices are similar to an ancient practice called *she'eilat chalom*, where one poses a question before sleeping in anticipation of receiving an answer in a dream. This technique is the subject of a book called *Questions and Answers from Heaven* by one of the *ba'alei haTosafot*.

During a desperate time in his life, King Saul sought answers in dreams, but he did not receive an answer (I Samuel 28:6). Rabbi Chaim Vital, the primary student of the Arizal, taught that this practice should only be attempted by those who properly prepare themselves and are spiritually worthy.

Whereas the *nefesh* is rooted primarily in the unconscious, instinctual level of soul and the *ruach* and *neshamah* are rooted in the more conscious levels of soul, the remaining two levels — *chayah* and *yechidah* — have their source in the superconscious levels of soul. It is at the level of *chayah*, the bridge between consciousness and superconsciousness, that Divine inspiration and prophecy begin to reveal themselves. Here is where the soul is in touch with its pure potential, and in the dream state it pushes to reveal itself in actuality. The two dreams of Joseph where he envisions himself as a leader were not egotistical flights of fantasy, as his brothers interpreted them, but rather prophetic views of his full potential.

Dreams at the level of *yechidah*, the root of the soul in its Divine source, are qualitatively different in that at the previous four levels the origin of dreams are from within a person, whereas at this level the origin is from God Above. It is at this level that dreams are messages and directives from God or predict events that are destined to unfold. Most of the Biblical dreams discussed in chapter 1 are in this category.

A beautiful allusion to the relationship between the level of *yechidah* and the other levels of soul can be found in the vowel called a *cholam*, whose letters are the very same as *chalom*, dream. The shape of the vowel, a dot hovering above the letter *vav*, ו, alludes to a separate level above the base form. The dot above alludes to prophetic dreams, while the *vav* symbolizes dreams produced by the relatively lower levels of soul.

To review the five levels of soul and their corresponding categories of dreams:

| Level of Soul | Type of Dream |
|---|---|
| Nefesh (instinct) | Result of physical conditions |
| Ruach (emotion) | Reaction to daily events |
| Neshamah (intellect) | Solution seeking |
| Chayah (bridge between the conscious and superconscious) | Vision of potential |
| Yechidah (unique divine soul) | Message from God |

It is important to realize that not all dreams fall neatly into just one of the categories described above. A dream may result from physical conditions and yet also be rooted in the events of the day and seek solutions at the same time. Or it may be rooted in one's pure potential, but be mired in unrectified emotions. A heavenly message or destined event may clothe itself in a dream from one of the lower levels. In short, the different combinations of input and the varied gradations of dreams are truly complex. A dream interpreter has to not only identify and match the symbols to the reality of the dreamer, but also to intuit the various sources in the soul from where the dream emanates.

The ladder of dreams stretches from the earth to the heights of heaven, from the most primal animal drives to the more lofty aspirations of the soul. Our dreams keep us aware of our frailties as well as of our potential. The purer our thoughts, speech, and actions, the clearer our dreams become. As in Jacob's dream, God is always found at the top of the ladder, calling us to fulfill our mission in this world.

5

# Dreams and the
# Mystery of Time

ho has not experienced the feeling of waking in the morning after a dream that seemed like days or years or lifetimes, or of dreaming of the same scene over and over and over again? Who has not sat in a class or lounged around his house and suddenly found his mind wandering to deeply painful or joyful memories of years gone by or tripping to the future through a carnival of fantasies and emotional roller coaster rides of the ego?

Sleep researchers say we dream but one to two hours a night and dream an average of four to seven dreams during that time. Yet most people spend that much time, or more, daydreaming every day. We actually dream every night, the only question is whether we remember our dreams or not. In fact, recordings of brain waves show our minds are even more active during sleep than during waking hours.

Not only dreams have the effect of distorting our usual perception of the constant flow of time. Reality as well is experienced through the subjectivity of time. Uneasy situations seem to "last forever," and whole summers can vanish "like a dream." Milestone occasions can feel like they will never arrive and peak moments can stay with us for eternity. The passing of time can be quite subjective and is very much dependent on consciousness.

As mentioned above, the letter *vav* in the Torah can transform past into future and future into past. The archetypal figures of the Bible are larger than life because their stories are ever present energies manifest in each and every person in every generation. The cycle of the Jewish year and the many rituals and symbols associated with the months, seasons, and holidays serve to bring both the past and the future into the present. The holidays are like vortex points of energy on an ever-ascending spiral. They arrive at the same point each year, but one notch higher on the spiral. In this way each point connects to the past as well as the future on the same axis.

The first mitzvah the Jewish people received as a nation was to designate the month of Nissan as the first of the months. At that time God taught Moses the order of the Jewish calendar and its secrets. A slave does not control time; only a free man can do so. The first mitzvah therefore relates to becoming a master of time, as that is the first step in the long road to true freedom.

All cycles of seven, especially Shabbat, are particularly wired to a Divine cycle of time. By engaging oneself completely in Shabbat one transcends the world of time, while continuing to operate in its strictures. A Yiddish expression describing these two experiences in time is "In the world and [simultaneously] out of the world" — a paradoxical yet attainable state of awareness. The ability to stop all one's weekday activities and dedicate a day to spiritual pursuits is crucial to becoming a master of time.

God, who creates and continually renews the world, including time, is the quintessential example of being simultaneously "in the world and out of the world." The four letters of God's name are the same letters which make up the Hebrew words for "past," "present," and "future." We experience time linearly, while for God all time is simultaneous.

Rebbe Nachman of Breslov in his classic work *Likkutei Moharan* (*Torah* 61:2) explains that we have a hard time conceiving God as being above time because of our relatively narrow awareness and intellect. The greater the conscious intellect, the more time is nullified for that person. In a dream state the conscious mind is no longer in control, and what remains is the pure power of imagination. That is why seventy years can go by in just fifteen minutes of dreaming. Yet to the one of even higher intellect those seventy years become like only fifteen minutes even while awake, as for him time is even more nullified. This process continues ad infinitim; as the intellect becomes more and more clarified, so too, does the power of imagination, with the result being the ever greater nullification of time.

About this very lofty level God spoke to David, saying: "Today I have given birth to you" (Psalms 2:7). The experience of viewing every moment as truly new, of being reborn at every moment, is true Messianic consciousness. David, from whom the Messiah will come, was, according to tradition, not allotted any time in this world. His entire life was experienced as if "today I have given birth to you," again and again. This helps explain how David reached such lofty heights of praise for God, as he experienced God's constant mercy and life-giving energy moment by moment.

Rabbi Nachman finishes his teaching by stating that the same dynamic holds true for space. The greater the intellect, the less space matters. One who reaches spiritual heights can thus traverse great distances in what seems like just a short time. In other words, the closer one comes to uniting with the essence of God, the more time and space become nullified before his or her will.

One of the most famous stories in the Talmud regarding dreams is that of Choni HaMe'agel (*Ta'anit* 23a). Choni was very puzzled by the verse, "When God returns the captivity of Zion, we will be as dreamers" (Psalms 126:1). "The captivity of Zion" refers to the Jewish people, who were taken to exile in Babylonia and did not return to the land of Israel for seventy years. How could it be, Choni wondered, that a people could sleep for seventy years and still survive?

One day he met a man planting a carob tree. Choni asked him how long the tree would take to bear fruit, and the man replied that it would take seventy years. Choni was incredulous and asked the man why he wanted to plant a tree whose fruit he would never taste. The man responded that his father had planted a tree for him, so he would plant a tree for his children.

Choni sat down and soon fell into a deep sleep. When he awoke, he saw someone gathering carobs from the very tree he had watched being planted. He asked the man if he had planted the tree and was told that his father's father had planted it. Choni then understood that he had been asleep for seventy years.

He returned to his home and asked if Choni's son was there. He was told that Choni's grandson now lived in the home. Choni then revealed who he was, but no one believed him. At the local house of study, Choni was treated like a stranger. Sad and dejected, Choni prayed to die and his prayer was answered.

Choni received his name "HaMe'agel" from an earlier incident, when in response to a very harsh drought he drew a circle — a *ma'agal* — and refused to move from it until God caused rain to fall. Both stories about Choni reveal his concern for the Jewish people, first in the immediate, practical sense when he prayed for rain, and then in the more futuristic, global sense, as he wondered how they could survive an exile of seventy years and future exiles as well.

The Maharsha explains the entire story as an allegory dealing with the reality of exile. The incident with the carob tree is a hopeful sign. Even though the carob tree would not give fruit for seventy years, the same length of time as the Babylonian exile, in the end it would bear fruit. This is a sign that all is not lost and that as harsh as exile is, future generations will thrive to the point where they cannot even relate to Choni, who represents the suffering of a previous era.

A beautiful allusion is found in the Hebrew word for carob, *charuv*, which has the same root as the word *churban*, "destruction." Though the carob tree may seem lifeless and destroyed for all those years, in truth it is growing in strength until the time will come for it to give forth its fruit. This is an allusion to the inner dynamics of exile, a period of spiritual hibernation that gives the appearance of sleep, but is really a time of quietly gathering one's strength until the time of redemption comes.

Choni's sleep of seventy years can be understood as him not only dreaming of what is on his mind but also trying to find hopeful solutions to the problems troubling him. Rebbe Nachman's example of a fifteen-minute dream seeming like seventy years fits in well with this story.

It is not just in the whimsical world of dreams or man's subjective perspective that time is elastic. Despite the long-held notion that the flow of time is constant under all circumstances, Albert Einstein proved that time in fact was not an absolute constant, but is affected by gravity and velocity. This has been shown many times by clocks sent into space and returning with a different time than earth time. As velocity approaches the speed of light, time slows dramatically until time as it were stops, and past and future merge into an eternal present.

This mystery of time is alluded to in the verse, "And Abraham was old, coming into days, and God blessed Abraham with everything" (Genesis 24:1). The word "old" refers to an advanced level of wisdom which Abraham reached, allowing him to transcend the normal strictures of time. "Coming into days" alludes to the World to Come, which is not just a future dimension reached after death or a new state of reality to be revealed after the advent of the Messianic era, but is a time that is always coming, the future already revealed in the present.

The key to Joseph's interpretations of the dreams of the butler, the baker, and Pharaoh was his ability to translate the physical objects and their numbers into periods of time. Rashi comments that the magicians of Pharaoh interpreted the seven cows and the seven kernels of wheat as the number of daughters he would father and subsequently bury, or the kingdoms he would conquer but then lose. Only Joseph could see the intrinsic connection between space and time.

Rabbi Yitzchak Ginsburgh explains that time is the inner dimension of space, in that all change to the three physical dimensions only occurs through time. The *Sefer Yetzirah* (3:3) discusses five dimensions: three of space, one of time, and one of soul. Science, which now posits time as well as space as dimensions, still has not reached the discovery of "soul," the divine dimension that gives life force to reality and fills it with a valued purpose. Even here, though, science recently has accepted the effect that consciousness has on reality, and it is probably only a matter of time before scientists will come to understand "soul" as a dimension as well.

Time serves as the intermediary between the dimensions of space and soul, between the physical world and the spiritual worlds. It assumes its role as intermediary due to the insurmountable "distance" between the infinite light of God and the finite physical worlds. If the light of God shone directly into the worlds, one of two things would happen: Either it would overwhelm the physical world and totally nullify it, or in order to prevent this it would become subservient to the lower worlds and would then lose its purpose for existing. Therefore, the light of God assumes a pulsating rhythm of "running and returning," at every moment both giving life to all the worlds and retreating in order not to overwhelm those same worlds. This dynamic, rhythmic current creates time where every pulsation is a "segment" of time. In this way time is the bridge connecting the dimensions of space to the dimension of soul (as taught by Rav Yitzchak Ginsburgh).

This very idea lies at the basic understanding of light being a stream of tiny packets or particles of light called photons. These tiny packets are called quanta, from which the term "quantum physics" is derived. One of the greatest paradoxes of science is that light acts as both a particle and a wave. This mystery of light is intrinsically connected to the mystery of time. Both light and time, which appear like constant flowing streams, are at their very essence Divine pulsating energy.

Joseph was able to see the inner essence of time enlivening the symbols in the dreams and interpret them accordingly. When interpreting the dreams of the butler and the baker, he interpreted the number three, which appeared in both their dreams, as days, while the number seven in the dreams of Pharaoh he interpreted as years. This also entailed a deep understanding of the symbolism of numbers.

Three relates to the three inner intellectual *sefirot*, the channels of Divine influx present at all levels of creation, while seven relates to the lower, more external *sefirot*, the emotional and behavioral characteristics. The intellect operates primarily in a private realm within a person, while human characteristics interact more with the outside world. Therefore, Joseph interpreted the number three as three days, in which the butler and baker's private fates would be determined, whereas with Pharaoh he saw the number seven as alluding to events taking place in the public arena over a longer period. The root of the word year, *shanah*, also means "change." Thus he intuited the seven lean cows consuming the seven fat cows as a process taking a longer period of time. He also knew the secret of the statement in the Midrash that the dream of a king is a dream for the whole world (B*ereishit Rabbah* 89:4).

The idea expressed above that the greater the intellect, the more time is nullified teaches us that the source of dreams in the subconscious and superconscious is from a higher level than normative consciousness. When we sleep, our normal level of cognizance makes way for the soul to free itself from the confines of the body and ordinary perceptions of time and space. Time is experienced so differently because higher levels of soul are not as bound to the normal boundaries of time and space.

Just as the body stays healthy by relieving itself of waste materials every day, so too, the different levels of soul need to "excrete" a myriad of stimulus from their midst in order to remain healthy. Although nightmares are scary, they serve the purpose of alerting the psyche to the fears and raw emotions bubbling below the surface. In this sense they are like a fever which is very cathartic to the body.

Then there are those special dreams where the soul soars upwards to its Godly source and approaches revelation of its Divine mission. In "real" time these dreams can last a matter of minutes, but the impression they leave on the soul can last a lifetime.

Our superconscious is rooted in a place above time, and our dreams mirror this like a clear mountain lake reflects its pristine surroundings.

6

# Prophetic Allusions

lthough prophecy ended long ago, the "shadow" of prophecy is still accessible, especially in our dreams. Almost everyone at some point dreams of events that subsequently happen. These occurrences fill us with wonder and awe. And it doesn't just happen in our dreams. How many times do we think of someone spontaneously and he or she calls a few minutes later, or we think of someone we haven't thought of in ages and upon returning home find a letter from him or her in the mail or the inbox? These eerie events give us the feeling that there is much more to life than what meets the eye.

Similar to dreams, which transcend time, prophecy entails the future being shown in the present. We have discussed how ultimately both the past and the future exist in the present. When God reveals future events to the prophet, the prophet is glimpsing the future (or a possible future) in the present. Most of the time, the soul is held down by the "gravity" of the body and earthly influences. But on occasion, when it manages to escape material bounds, either consciously or unconsciously, the soul can access a matrix where all dimensions are ever present.

We saw how all the dreams in the Bible are messages from God. Sometimes the message is quite clear and unambiguous, while other times the information is coded in allegory and symbols. Moses alone communicated with God "face to face"; all the other prophets received their prophecies in visions and dreams. For the prophet these messages were very much like dreams in that they needed to be interpreted. Those prophets who succeeded in developing their powers of imagination and intellect properly were able to correctly interpret the signs and symbols.

In the first chapter of the book of Jeremiah, God informs Jeremiah that he has been chosen to be a prophet to the nations. Like so many other Jewish leaders, Jeremiah professes inadequacy for the task. In a beautiful exchange, God teaches Jeremiah the secret of interpreting prophecy:

> The word of God came to me, saying, "What do you see, Jeremiah?" I said, "I see the staff of an almond tree." Then God said to me, "You have seen well; for I will hasten My word to perform it."
>
> The word of God came to me a second time, saying, "What do you see?" I said, "I see a boiling pot, and its spout is facing north." Then God said to me, "Out of the north the evil shall break forth upon all the inhabitants of the land."
>
> (Jeremiah 1:11–14)

This exchange teaches us that Jeremiah was in fact able to receive the images God was sending him and God was teaching him how to interpret the signs. In the first case the allusion is quite subtle. The Hebrew word for almond, *shakeid*, shares the same root as the word "to hasten," and in fact the almond receives its name from being the very first fruit tree to blossom in Israel each spring. The interpretation of the image shown to Jeremiah was based on a deep understanding of the Hebrew language and of its role as a conduit for symbolic association.

Earlier in this book we mentioned that a good part of the Talmud's discussions on dream interpretation revolve around explanations of what specific objects, places, characters, words, and books mean if seen in a dream. Among this list are many examples of symbols being interpreted according to their Hebrew names, much as in the case of Jeremiah and the almond tree.

No matter how universal a symbol may be, every individual may have a different feeling toward it. Nonetheless, the Sages wanted to impart the idea that certain symbols seen in dreams have a universal connotation. Around 1,500 years after this concept was codified in the Talmud, modern psychology began to develop the same concept.

Rabbi Yochanan taught that three types of dreams are fulfilled: a dream seen in the early morning, a dream one's friend has of him, and a dream that is interpreted within a dream (*Berachot* 55b). The Maharsha explains that an early morning dream is less apt to be the product of the mind replaying events of the day, as those images would have already run their course during the early night's dreams. A dream about someone else is also less likely to be a product of one's own thoughts, as people think more about themselves than about others.

Other Sages added a dream that is repeated to the list of dreams likely to be fulfilled. This is based on Joseph's statement to Pharaoh that the reason he dreamt two very similar dreams in one night was because it was a sign that God was hastening to fulfill them (Genesis 41:32).

Another teaching of Rabbi Yochanan is very significant in understanding prophecy today. He states: "If one awoke and a verse from Torah fell into his mouth, this is minor prophecy" (*Berachot* 55b). This statement corresponds to the idea that dreams are one-sixtieth of prophecy and that minor prophecy still exists, long after the era of the prophets.

# Prophetic Allusions in the Torah

In addition to prophetic dreams and the words of the prophets, the Torah is replete with subtle allusions to future events and descriptions of future occurrences. The book of Deuteronomy teaches that if the Jewish people listen to the word of God, observe the mitzvot, and act justly, God will reward them with peace and prosperity in the Land of

Israel. If, however, they do not listen and observe, they will experience military defeat and a long and cruel exile. The Torah describes the horrors of exile in frightening detail. Anyone even superficially knowledgeable of Jewish history can recognize how everything predicted in the Torah has come to pass.

Although the jury is still out regarding what are commonly called the "Bible Codes," computers have revealed truly amazing mathematical patterns in the verses of the Torah that were never previously comprehended. These patterns reveal hidden messages, mathematical symmetry, and infinite layers of meaning in the Torah, ideas that lie at the basis of *sod*, the secret Kabbalistic tradition.

The role of the prophet in Biblical times was well established. Prophets led the people of Israel until the establishment of the Davidic Dynasty, and even afterwards had a major role in the nation's leadership. Although prophets were occasionally despised or hounded for their predictions of dire events that would take place if the people didn't change their ways, they wielded great power and authority. Of course, power corrupts in the hands of the wrong people and there were always those who wielded this power for selfish reasons or who pretended to be prophets when they really were not. Nonetheless, the true prophets of Israel commanded great respect and led the people in their service of God. Their prophecies of the future Messianic days have provided hope and comfort for generations of Jews and have influenced and inspired people of many religions. To this day their words are studied and read publicly in the synagogue, and they continue to have an enormous impact on people throughout the world.

Just as a "negative dream suffices for it," meaning that the scare one receives from a frightening dream is sometimes enough punishment or incentive to change, the dire predictions of the prophets could serve the same purpose if the people changed their ways. We are taught that negative prophecies do not have to happen, while the good prophecies recorded in the Bible will all eventually take place (Rambam, *Hilchot Yesodei HaTorah* 10:4). Negative prophecies did not negate the possibility of free choice and the rectifying power of positive change.

On a more subtle level, the Torah is filled with descriptions of events that are replete with prophetic allusion to future dynamics in Jewish history. When Rebecca experienced a turbulent pregnancy, she sought an explanation for her troubles from God. Rashi explains that she went to Shem, the son of Noah, who was a prophet. "And God said to her: 'Two nations are in your womb; two peoples from your insides will be separated. One people shall be stronger than the other, and the elder shall serve the younger' " (Genesis 25:23). Not only were these words prophetic in regard to the twins Jacob and Esau, whom she bore, but they were also prophetic of the complex relationship between the Jewish people, descendants of Jacob, and the Roman Empire, which according to tradition descends from Esau. The entire story of Jacob and Esau contains within it the seeds of the history that was later to unfold.

When Jacob sent Joseph to check on the welfare of his brothers who were pasturing sheep, the verse states that he sent him from "the valley of Hebron." Rashi points out that Hebron is not deep like a valley, but in the mountains. The verse, he explains, means that Jacob sent his son from the "deep design" of Abraham who was buried in Hebron, in order to fulfill that which God had told Abraham that his inheritors would be strangers and oppressed in a foreign land, but would leave with great wealth (*Rashi* on Genesis 37:14; *Sotah* 11a).

When Jacob sent his sons to Egypt to buy grain during the famine, his command was to "go down" (Genesis 42:2). These words were prophetic on two levels. First, they foretold the Jewish people's descent into slavery, and second, as Rashi points out, the numerical value of the word "go down," *redu*, is 210, the same number of years that the Jewish people were actually in Egypt!

Was Jacob conscious that his words to "go down" were prophetic, or was he unknowingly the channel for a prophetic statement? When he sent Joseph to check on his brothers, was he fully aware of the wheels he was setting in motion, or was he a vessel through which God was fulfilling the Jewish people's destiny? We can ask the same about ourselves, albeit on a lower level. Are we always aware of how we are agents for energies and dynamics beyond our conscious awareness? The answers to these questions touch the heart of the paradox of how free will and Divine providence operate simultaneously.

We can answer these questions with a discussion in the *Zohar*. Rabbi Chiya and Rabbi Yosei asked Rabbi Shimon Bar Yochai if the statement that "a dream not interpreted is like a letter not read" means that the dream is not fulfilled or that it is fulfilled without the dreamer knowing it. He answered them that it is fulfilled, but the dreamer is not aware of it. This is due to the fact that God does not act in the world before first revealing His actions to a prophet; and if there is no prophet He reveals His actions to a wise one; and otherwise He reveals it in a dream (*Zohar* I 183a–b).

After the death of Joseph, the Torah states: "A new king arose in Egypt who did not know Joseph" (Exodus 1:8). Rashi brings two opinions from the Talmud regarding the meaning of this verse: one is that it was a new king, while the other is that it was the same king, but he made new decrees. Rashi continues by explaining that it wasn't that the new king didn't know Joseph, but rather he made himself as if he didn't know him. No matter whether it was the same king or a different king, in both cases he pretended not to know or remember how Joseph had saved Egypt, and the whole world, from starvation. This incident and attitude has been played out countless times in innumerable places in Jewish history: Jews are invited into a kingdom, province, or country and work hard to become an integral part of the success of that society, only to face eventual jealousy and hatred, leading to pogroms and expulsion. When the time was convenient, they suddenly "didn't know Joseph."

The above examples of prophetic statements are but a drop in the bucket regarding prophecy in the Torah. One final example, though, will shed great light on the connection of dreams to prophecy. Among the eight special garments of the high priest, one of them was the breastplate of judgment. It was made of cloth and folded into a square that had a pouch. On the breastplate were twelve stones with the names of the tribes engraved on them and in the pouch was placed the mysterious *urim* and *tumim*, a parchment upon which was written the Ineffable Name of God (Exodus 28:15–30). The word *urim* is related to the word for light and *tumim* comes from the word "complete."

For as long as this breastplate of judgment was in Jewish hands, questions of great import would be submitted to the high priest and he would ask God for an answer. If he was worthy, the *urim* would light up letters of the names of the tribes, and the *tumim* would arrange the letters in order to spell out the answer. The high priest would then have to properly interpret the arrangement of the letters in order to understand the true message, much as a dream needs to be understood through interpretation. This is another deep connection between dreams and the Hebrew letters which we discussed earlier and which we will mention in coming chapters as well.

Another beautiful connection between dreams and prophecy relating to the breastplate is found in the names of two of the twelve precious stones. One stone was a diamond, *yahalom*, and another was *achlamah*, a jasper. Both of these words are very close to the word for dreams, *chalom* (as taught by Rav Yitzchak Ginsburgh).

A further association to dreams is found in the name of the breastplate of judgment itself, *choshen hamishpat*. When the letters of *choshen* are rearranged they spell "*nachash*," snake. The snake represents the characteristic of unrectified imagination and the false judgment which follows. This is seen clearly in the story of the Garden of Eden, where the snake causes doubt and temptation by urging Eve to eat of the Tree of Knowledge of Good and Evil. In addition, the snake represents desire and lust on many different levels. These bad qualities cloud judgment, causing uncertainty and guessing.

One of the magical practices forbidden by the Torah is sorcery, whose Hebrew root is the same as *nichush*, "guessing." This is explained to be a belief in superstitions upon which decisions are based. The idea of guessing means that without a proper sense of judgment one grabs for all sorts of omens and signs with which to make decisions. This is akin to the soul groping in the dark, only guessing where it is.

Paradoxically, it is Joseph, the master of dreams, who said to his brothers who did not recognize him: "Do you not realize that such a man as I can certainly divine (*nacheish yenacheish*)?" (Genesis 44:15). The word for "divine" in this verse is also from the root of *nachash*. When the power of imagination is refined and rectified, as Joseph's was, it raises the qualities of the *nachash* to manifest in positive pursuits, leading ultimately to Divine inspiration.

The numerical value of *nachash*, snake, is 358, identical to the value of Mashiach, the Messiah. The Messiah represents the force that is the complete opposite of that of the snake, though the fact that their numerical equivalent is equal hints to a common energy source. The Messiah will have the power to uplift and transform the energy of the snake for the good, paving the way for all humanity to follow in his footsteps.

The Tree of Life and the Tree of Knowledge of Good and Evil were both placed in the middle of the Garden of Eden and in fact shared the same roots.* The Messiah will inaugurate a new unified human consciousness where the soul and body will no longer work at cross-purposes. He will elevate and transform the source of dreams in the soul to a new perception of reality.

---

\* Rabbi Yitzchak Ginsburgh, *Consciousness and Choice* (Jerusalem: Gal Einai, 2004), p. 40.

7

# Dreams, Reality, and Torah

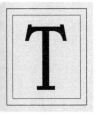hroughout this book we have seen the profound inter-connectedness of dreams, reality, and Torah. In the perception of time, in the manifestation of prophecy, and in the cardinal role and purpose of symbolism, these three realms merge and converge continually. Especially in the realm of the soul and consciousness, the lines are so often blurred as to be nonexistent. Where one begins and the other ends is far from clear.

We will return to a verse we have quoted a number of times in order to glean from it one more perspective. "A Song of Ascents: When God will return the captivity of Zion, we will be as dreamers" (Psalms 126:1). The Radak comments that when the redemption comes we will wake up as from a bad dream. In other words, the exile is compared to a bad dream, whereas redemption is a state of wakefulness. Rabbi Samson Raphael Hirsch adds an interesting viewpoint: When the people of Israel are in exile they are like dreamers who are out of touch with reality. Only when the redemption comes will Israel awake and realize how much and how deeply they influenced all the nations during their journeys in exile.

The Malbim explains just the opposite — the redemption will be like a dream come true in comparison to the harsh reality of the exile. All the years of dreaming of redemption will turn into reality.

Rabbi Yitzchak Ginsburgh states that along with the more normative explanation of exile being a state of sleep, as alluded to in the verse in Song of Songs: "I am asleep [in exile], but my heart is awake [longing for redemption]" (Songs of Songs 5:2), an even deeper Chassidic teaching is that the time of redemption will be such a miraculous dream that it will be beyond whatever the mind can fathom now. For the redemption will be a time when all paradoxes will be fully understood and revealed.

As proof that dreams are the products of one's own thoughts, the Talmud states that one never dreams of something totally impossible like "an elephant entering into the eye of a needle" (*Berachot* 55b). Rabbi Ginsburgh states that at the time of the final redemption, it will be possible for an elephant to enter through the eye of a needle, something which today seems the epitome of absurdity (*The Hebrew Letters*, pp. 288–89). This means that at the time of redemption that which is infinite will be revealed within the context of the finite. This is the metaphor of an elephant fitting through the eye of a needle.

As always, these two seemingly opposite opinions as to which state of being — exile or redemption — is a dream and which is reality are both correct. There obviously is an element in each that can be compared to being asleep and dreaming, and an element in each that can be compared to being awake. Many poets and writers throughout the ages have used the metaphor of people living their lives as if perpetually asleep and dreaming. For those who have ever had periods in life when they felt totally uninspired and bored by their work, their relationships, and their prospects in life, this metaphor is not far off the mark. This also applies to those who daydream endlessly of desires they will never fulfill, of places they will never go, and of goals they will never accomplish — for them life can seem like a bad dream.

A beautiful example of this notion is expressed by the poet Edgar Allan Poe:

*I stand amid the roar*
*Of a surf-tormented shore,*
*And I hold within my hand*
*Grains of the golden sand —*
*How few! Yet how they creep*
*Through my fingers to the deep,*
*While I weep — while I weep!*
*O God! Can I not grasp*
*Them with a tighter grasp?*
*O God! Can I not save*
*One from the pitiless wave?*
*Is all we see or seem*
*But a dream within a dream?**

Then there are those who dream and work to make their dreams come true, turning fanciful visions into the nuts and bolts of reality. For those who are inspired and believe that dreams come true, no aspiration is unreachable. Their dreams are more "real" than real, as they draw on an ideal future vision and make it real in the here and now. Rabbi Shlomo Carlebach always taught the importance of not letting go of your dreams; of believing in your potential and your highest visions and ideals and having the guts to realize them in the here and now.

The dreams of a person on a very lofty spiritual level, especially if consciously directed before sleep, can tune him into planes of reality just as real as what we call reality from our lower perspective. Jewish tradition, prayers, and text are replete with reference to angels, holy beings, spiritual worlds, and unseen dimensions. Some of these ideas, which were once thought of by science as figments of the imagination and poetic license, are now the subject of modern quantum physics and cosmology text books, albeit in a different language. The concepts of time as a dimension, black holes, parallel universes, time dilation, and

---

* Edgar Allan Poe, "A Dream within a Dream," *Poe: Selected Prose and Poetry* (New York: Rinehart & Co., 1959), p. 482.

the theory of relativity all stretch the imagination and in many cases fly in the face of logic, yet have been proven over and over in the laboratory. Our concept of reality today is what science fiction writers a hundred years ago were dreaming about.

When analyzing the word for dream, *chalom*, by each of its letters we saw how the letter *lamed*, the tallest of the letters, represented the aspiration of the heart. A well-known saying from the Sages is: "A person should always say to himself, 'When will my actions reach the level of the patriarchs, Abraham, Isaac, and Jacob?' " (*Tanna D'Bei Eliyahu* 25). Every Jew should aspire and dream about acquiring the soul aspects that made our patriarchs so elevated and holy.

There is a Chassidic custom, practiced by some, to recite the following words when waking in the morning from a dream: "Dream or reality?" The numerical value of that statement in Hebrew, *chalom o metziut*, equals exactly the names of the patriarchs. The question is if our striving to be like our great ancestors is real or just a fleeting wish that vanishes in the morning like a forgotten dream. On a deeper level, it is not so much if our dreams are real, it is whether we have the courage and fortitude to make our dreams reality.

The metaphor of life as "dream or reality," which was heard from Rabbi Yitzchak Ginsburgh, takes on a new perspective according to a teaching of Rabbi Isaac of Homil, a great Chassidic teacher. Based on Kabbalistic ideas he states that Adam Kadmon, "primordial man," the name of the very highest of spiritual worlds, is in a dream state, that is, this primordial level of the Divine creative process is in a superconscious state of "dreaming." On a deeper mystical level it could be said that all existence is happening in God's "head," that all that exists is the "dream" of God.

The word *kadmon*, primordial, equals 200, the same as the letter *reish*, which means "head." *Adam Kadmon* represents in the highly symbolic language of Kabbalah the primordial source of the ideal plan of Creation while still within God's thoughts, as it were. As a person first visualizes that which he wants to build or accomplish, and only later finds the practical means to bring his vision or dream into reality, so too, as it were, God first envisions creation deep within His infinite being and will, and only later implements His vision to create. Creation, then, is the actualization of the primordial dream of God, and all history is the actualizing process of transmuting that dream into reality.

The blueprint and plan for creation is both hidden and revealed in the Torah, the express reflection of the Divine will. The Hebrew word for world, *olam*, comes from the root that means "to hide." Paradoxically, the world is both the revelation of God and the hiding of God within nature. The last two letters of *chalom* are the same as the last two letters of *olam*, the root for world and hiding. As life is an ongoing process and cycle of revelation and hiddenness, so too dreams both reveal and hide meaning.

Spiritual growth depends on revealing that which is hidden and finding God in every situation and moment of life. God speaks to us within the essence of our souls, through the Torah we learn, by way of the circumstances of our lives, and in the images of our dreams. By envisioning and dreaming of a perfected future, the purpose of each individual, and all of creation, we manifest that dream in reality. By uniting our thoughts, speech, and deeds with the will of God, we enable the dream of God to come true.

# Part II
# The Dream of Jacob

8

# An Introduction to Jacob's Dream

erhaps the dream that has most captured the imagination of people around the world is the dream of Jacob seeing angels ascending and descending on a ladder reaching the heavens. Whereas most other Biblical dreams are associated with specific events, messages, or warnings, the dream of Jacob has an eternal, universal aspect which sets it in a category of its own. The story of Jacob's dream takes relatively few verses, yet millions of words have been written about it.

We discussed earlier the power and significance of symbolism. The lasting quality of a symbol lies in its ability to transcend the confines of time, lending itself to new and deeper associations in every generation. In many cases the simpler the symbolism, the more can be read into it.

This is certainly true with Jacob's dream, and it is for this reason that we have chosen it as an example of how to apply what we have presented in the first part of this book in a more in-depth fashion. We will now analyze many commentaries that have been written about the dream over the ages, as well as examine the dream in light of the ladder of dreams we constructed earlier in this book.

We hope that at the end of this book you will be inspired to delve more deeply into the subject and find new relevance in it so that the dream will speak directly to you in the here and now.

# The Context of Jacob's Dream

Jacob went from Beer Sheba, and he went towards Haran. And he came upon the place and slept there, for the sun had set. He took of the stones of the place and placed them around his head, and he lay down to sleep in that place.

And he dreamt, and behold a ladder was set in the earth and its head reached the heavens, and behold, angels of God were ascending and descending on it.

And behold God was standing over him, and He said, "I am God, God of your father Abraham and God of Isaac. The ground upon which you are lying I will give to you and to your descendants. Your descendants will be as numerous as the dust of the earth, and you will spread out to the west, to the east, to the north, and to the south. And all the families of the earth shall bless themselves by you and by your offspring. Behold, I am with you; I will guard you wherever you go, and I will return you to this soil, for I will not forsake you until I have done what I have spoken about you."

Jacob awoke from his sleep and said, "Surely God is in this place, and I did not know!" And he became frightened and said, "How awesome is this place! This is none other than the house of God, and this is the gate of the heavens!"

Jacob arose in the morning and he took the stone that he had placed around his head and set it up as a pillar, and he poured oil on its top. And he named the place Beit-El, although Luz had been the city's name originally.

(Genesis 28:10–19)

Rabbi Shlomo ben Chafni, a well-known scholar in the Babylonian academy of Sura a thousand years ago, explained that to accurately interpret a dream it is critical to know the context of the dream (Rabbi Shlomo Ben Chafni, *Pitron HaChalomot*, pp. 75–76). Among the important factors to know are where the dreamer lives, was he sick or well at the time of the dream, what he ate the night of the dream, if there were recent deaths or traumatic events in his life, the events of the days leading up to the dream, and at what point of the night he had the dream. Each of these factors could help explain the images and symbols in the dream. Therefore, to understand Jacob's dream, it is imperative to know what was happening in Jacob's life at the time of the dream.

The story of the dream begins with the verse, "And Jacob went out from Beer Sheba, and he went towards Haran" (Genesis 28:10). The Beit HaLevi comments that a person who is traveling usually does so in order to either leave a previous situation or enter a new one. In this verse, both the point of departure and the final destination are mentioned to inform us that Jacob had two intentions in traveling: to escape the wrath of Esau for having "stolen" his blessing and to go to Haran to fulfill his parents' requests that he find a wife among his mother's family.

Both of these reasons are crucial to understanding what was on Jacob's mind as he lay down to sleep the night of the dream. Tradition teaches that Jacob actually spent fourteen years in the academy of Shem and Ever between leaving Beer Sheba and lying down to sleep on the night of his dream (*Bereishit Rabbah* 68:11), but it is certain that the trauma of having to flee his own brother was still very much on his mind. We will see this idea developed further when analyzing the symbolism of the dream and comparing it with his final confrontation with Esau twenty years later.

In addition to fleeing his brother, Jacob was going to Haran with the purpose of marrying and raising a family. Unlike ordinary mortals, Jacob's sole intent in marrying was to continue the heritage entrusted to him by his parents — to build the family that would be the cornerstone of the future Jewish people. To do this, he had to leave the protected environment of the house of study for the first time and immerse himself in the more mundane world, spending his time earning a living and interacting with less than honest people.

Rebbe Natan, the primary student of Rebbe Nachman of Breslov, explains the inner meaning of the opening verse in the following manner. Beer Sheba literally means "the well of seven." The number seven in Torah represents cycles of time and the concept of progress. Jacob leaving Beer Sheba represents his desire to attain a higher spiritual level, to go to the next phase of his life. The word *Haran*, his destination, means anger, or the obstacles confronting one who attempts to raise him- or herself to a new level of spirituality. In other words, any time we seek to reach a higher level of spiritual attainment, we must be prepared to confront a whole new configuration of forces that will attempt to prevent us from achieving our goal. No matter how high a level of spirituality we reach, it is no panacea for the obstacles we must cross to go further.

This, according to Rebbe Natan, was the situation Jacob faced in his life at the time of the dream, a teaching relevant for each and every person. Rather than being discouraged by knowing this spiritual law, we can actually be strengthened, as we can anticipate obstacles and face them without fear, knowing they are a sign of spiritual progress (*Torat Natan, Parashat Vayeitzei*).

This idea can be applied to each week of seven days in microcosm. As we leave each Shabbat with new inspiration and peace of mind, we are immediately confronted with the new challenges of the coming week. All week we strive to accomplish our work despite the inevitable daily obstacles and encounters. The harder we work, both physically and spiritually, the more rewarding and peaceful is the next Shabbat. In this sense the ladder in Jacob's dream is like the week and God standing over him at the top of the ladder is comparable to Shabbat.

Another allusion in the opening verse of this section relates to Beer Sheba, "the well of seven." A well is a pit that is dug deep in the earth in order to draw forth water. The Talmud teaches that any mention of water in the Bible is an allusion to Torah (*Bava Kamma* 17a). A ladder, on the other hand, reaches upward towards heaven. In spiritual terms there is a correlation between the two symbols of the well and the ladder. The deeper one delves into the living waters of the Torah, the higher one climbs in his or her goal to be close to God. The higher the soul reaches towards union with God, the deeper one is able to integrate the Torah he or she learns.

Jacob left Beer Sheba in order to strike out on his own. Both Abraham and Isaac dug wells before him and now it was his turn. These wells symbolize their digging their roots deeply into the Land of Israel and revealing new waters of revelation in the world. It is significant that after his dream Jacob comes upon a well that is covered with a large stone. The shepherds tell him they cannot remove the stone until all of them assemble, as it is too heavy. Upon seeing Rachel for the first time, Jacob proceeds to remove the stone by himself. This represents Jacob coming into his own, as he was now ready to assume his role as the next patriarch (Genesis 29:1–12).

# The Prayer in "the Place"

The next verse in the story of the dream relates, "And he [Jacob] came upon the place and slept there, for the sun had set. He took from the stones of the place and placed them around his head, and he lay down to sleep in that place" (Genesis 28:11). The word "he came upon," *vayifga*, is interpreted by the Sages to mean "he prayed," due to its usage in other places. This verse serves as the precedent for the evening prayer, which was established by Jacob (*Berachot* 26b).

Jacob's prayer is highly significant because prayer is crucial in order to overcome the inevitable obstacles that get in the way of spiritual advancement. The fact that Jacob prayed at night represents his turning to God even in the midst of darkness and uncertainty. It is paradoxical that the very times when we need most to reach out to God for help are the times when it is the hardest to do so, due to feelings of depression, sadness, or futility. Jacob's presence of mind in turning to God at night when things got tough serves as a precedent for Jews in every time and place.

"The place" Jacob came upon was Mount Moriah, the future site of the Temple, the same place where Abraham bound Isaac to the altar (*Rashi, Genesis* 28:11). The same word, *bamakom*, was used when God commanded Abraham to take Isaac to be bound "on one of the mountains that I will tell you" (Genesis 22:2). As Abraham approached the mountain, it is written: "On the third day he lifted up his eyes and saw the place from afar" (ibid., 4). The *Zohar* explains that the third day mentioned in this verse is a hint to Jacob, the third of the patriarchs. For three days Abraham was walking with the burden of contradiction upon him. God had fulfilled His promise to give him a son who would inherit the land and continue the spiritual path Abraham had blazed, and now the same God had just commanded him to offer his son as a sacrifice. Then Abraham saw the place from afar and had a prophetic glimpse of Jacob, the future descendant of Isaac. This heartened him, revealing that in the end all would be resolved.

"For the sun had set" is interpreted by the Midrash to mean that it set before its time; God arranged that Jacob would sleep on Mount Moriah as this was the place where he was destined to have his dream (*Bereishit Rabbah* 68:10). (There is some disagreement among the Sages about the actual identity of this place, and not all agree that it was actually Mount Moriah. This matter will be discussed in greater depth further on.)

Another explanation of the sun setting relates to the trials and tests in a person's life. When God tests an individual, his previous spiritual level and clarified intellect are diminished in order that he be tested, that is, challenged to rise to the occasion and in so doing attain an even higher level of consciousness. The Slonimer Rebbe explains that if this temporary diminishment would not occur, how would it be a test? This prerequisite for a test is alluded to in the sun setting before its time, forcing Jacob to begin digging deeper inside for the faith and fortitude he would need in his new stage of life (*Netivot Shalom, Vayeira*, p. 120).

The setting of the sun as a metaphor for the diminishment of consciousness also relates to dreams. When we go to sleep or begin to daydream, our normative intellect fades into the background as the subconscious powers of the soul become more prominent. Although the intellect is still active in dream states (as is the subconscious active in wake states), the dream state can be compared to the setting of the intellect, a diminishment of intelligence and consciousness.

# The Stones of the Place

The last action taken by Jacob before he slept was to arrange stones around his head. Rashi comments that this was to protect him from wild animals. We can further say that Jacob was aware that he was leaving not only family and mentors but also, for the first time, the Land of Israel. He took the stones "of the place," of the Land of Israel, and placed them around his head as a symbolic act of protection. Even as he left the land for unknown destinations and possible dangers, the holiness of the land would go with him.

According to tradition Jacob placed twelve stones around his head, symbolizing his destiny to give birth to the twelve tribes. Rashi notes that the verse after the dream states: "Jacob arose in the morning and he took *the stone* that he had placed around his head…" (Genesis 28:16). Rashi quotes the midrash, which states that all of the stones argued with each other over which one would have the merit of Jacob lying on it, so God fused them together into one stone. This signifies the unity of the Jewish people and their unique mission of revealing the oneness of God in the world.

Rashi notes that the Torah states, "He lay down to sleep in that place," which connotes that he lay down there, but not in other places. This teaches that Jacob never slept the whole night during his fourteen years in the academy of Shem and Ever. Rather, he would sleep for very short spells, just enough to renew himself before continuing his studies (*Bereishit Rabbah* 68:11). This practice was also followed by King David, who awoke at midnight each night and spent the rest of the night studying, praying, meditating, and playing music in praise of God (*Berachot* 3b).

A result of Jacob not sleeping all those years could be that he had not experienced or confronted a certain level of subconscious in many years. The first time he slept so deeply, the Torah records his dream. As we have discussed, dreams are critical to mental health. They release the subconscious fears and conflicts buried deep inside and create an avenue for dealing with issues that need to be addressed.

Another explanation of the symbolism of the stones relates to the Hebrew letters. *Sefer Yetzirah*, one of the oldest books of Kabbalah in existence, states that God created the universe with thirty-two pathways of wisdom (*Sefer Yetzirah* 1:1). These pathways are the twenty-two Hebrew letters and the ten *sefirot*, the Divine channels of energy that serve as the conduits of creation, as well as the archetypal models of all physical and spiritual processes. In this sense, the letters are considered the building blocks of creation, as the *Sefer Yetzirah* further states: "Twenty-two foundation letters: He engraved them, He carved them, He permuted them, He weighed them, He transformed them, and with them He depicted all that was formed and all that would be formed" (ibid. 2:2).

In a later chapter of *Sefer Yetzirah* we find the following enigmatic statement: "Two stones build two houses, three stones build six houses, four stones build twenty-four houses, five stones build one hundred and twenty houses, six stones build six hundred and twenty houses, seven stones build five thousand and forty houses. From here on, go out and calculate that which the mouth cannot speak and the ear cannot hear" (ibid. 4:16).

An Introduction to Jacob's Dream • 93

The commentators explain that the stones represent Hebrew letters and the houses are words built from letters. When permuting letters, one can build two words from two letters, six words from three letters, and so on. Permutation of letters in a word yields great insight into the meaning of the word and its broader scope of associations. (The *Tikunei Zohar*, an ancient Kabbalistic text, applies this idea to the first word of the Torah, *bereishit*, "in the beginning," in order to reveal profound secrets of Creation and the Divine creative process.) The stones of Jacob's dream, therefore, can be understood as symbolizing the Hebrew letters, the building blocks of Creation.

In the first chapter of this book we explained briefly the connection between dreams and the Hebrew letters. Man's thought process, both conscious and subconscious, can be seen as the mind being bombarded with a constant stream of stimuli and information. The first stage of intelligence is creating a logical order from the initial flood of input. The stimuli, or "letters," enter the mind in a random, nonsensical order. The mind then begins to take the individual "stones" or letters and commences to build "houses" or words. These words create thoughts, which are still pure potential at this state. They become actualized and concrete through speech and action. This actualization process is alluded to in the word for stone, *even*, being a combination of the words *av* and *ben*, father and son. As a son is hidden in potential within the seed of the father, so too, words and actions are hidden within the pure potential of thought. Just as the Hebrew letters are conceived of as the building blocks of creation, so too are they the building blocks of the thought process of man.

The subconscious, though, seems to have a sense of order and logic quite different from the intellect and normative consciousness. In fact, through the lens of the intellect, the subconscious, as it manifests in dreams, appears to be in a state of dissonance and disorder, yet this is not necessarily true. The subconscious simply transcends ordinary logic and has an order all its own. Yet the order ultimately depends on what is fueling the subconscious. When it is being given life force from an unrectified sense of imagination, the animal soul, and ego-driven emotions, the subconscious tends to be chaotic and disturbing. This leads to the type of dream that the prophets and Sages taught should be discarded. On the other hand, when the subconscious is being nourished by the higher levels of soul, its creative tendencies give birth to Divine inspiration and prophecy.

Unfettered by the persona, the psychological term for the face or mask that we don in public, the subconscious in dreams permutes the "letters" of the circumstances and feelings of the dreamer into a composite collage, full of pomp and theatrical flair. Yet this dramatic expression of events and sentiment is many times a more accurate reflection of our true feelings than the veneer of public correctness is.

A beautiful allusion to the correspondence between the Hebrew letters and dreams is gleaned from the Hebrew word for "he lay down to sleep," וישכב, which can be divided into ויש כ״ב, "and there are twenty-two [Hebrew letters]." Interpreting dreams is a process of building meaning, symbolized by houses, from various symbols, symbolized by letters.

Rabbi Yitzchak Ginsburgh explains that when the Jewish people are in exile, their souls are asleep. The same applies to an individual in spiritual exile. Rabbi Ginsburgh relates this sleeping state to a verse in Psalms, "Our signs we did not see" (Psalms 74:9). The word for "signs" in this verse means wonders and miracles of Divine providence, as well as letters. When the soul is asleep, deadened by exile, the letters and signs in its dreams are chaotic and disordered, a reflection of the soul's confused state. Spiritual redemption is reflected in a higher order of logic being revealed through dreams.*

Even worse than just being asleep is not remembering one's dreams, thus losing touch with one's ultimate purpose. The Talmud goes so far as to state that one who goes seven days without dreaming is called "evil" (*Berachot* 14a). Rashi explains that a person who is spiritually fit would not be ignored by Heaven. Therefore, not dreaming for

---

* Rabbi Yitzchak Ginsburgh, *My Heart is Asleep But My Heart Is Awake* (Jerusalem: Gal Einai Publications, 1996).

seven days is an indication of a low spiritual level.

Jacob lay down to sleep that night chased by his past, driven towards an unknown future. He was full of trust and doubt, confidence and uncertainty, hope and foreboding. He stood between the world he knew so well and the world he was destined to conquer; between existential loneliness and finding his soul mate. He had received the blessing of Abraham, and the weight of that inheritance, from his father. He stood in the shadow of his father and grandfather, both spiritual giants, as he attempted to forge his own appointed path. Ultimately Jacob's conflicts are our conflicts, his longings and hopes are our challenges, and his struggles paved the way for our struggles. The dream of Jacob is our dream, our reality, our destiny.

# 9

# Symbolic Elements of Jacob's Dream

And he dreamt and behold a ladder was set in the earth and its head reached the heavens, and behold, angels of God were ascending and descending on it.

(Genesis 28:12)

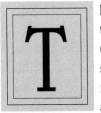

his verse is so pregnant with symbolism and meaning that we have dedicated most of the rest of the book to understanding its many messages. Although the message God imparted to Jacob during the dream is of primary importance, the image of the ladder and the angels ascending and descending are not just casual props or background frills to the dream, but are part of an even deeper message being revealed to him. This is the secret of symbols — their outer finite form contains eternal significance and endless shades of meaning.

The letters of the Hebrew word for ladder, *sulam*, can be permuted to form the word *semel*, which means "symbol." This beautiful allusion sheds light on the question of why this image has captured the world's imagination for the millennia. The ladder in Jacob's dream is so powerful a symbol because hidden in its very name is the entire concept of symbolism!

The fact that the ladder is described as being firmly grounded in the earth while its head reached the heavens accentuates the idea of the ladder being a connecting force between earth and heaven. We are taught that the creation of heaven and earth in the first verse of the Torah was an all-encompassing creation. The term "heaven" refers to all spiritual entities and worlds, while the term "earth" refers to all physical matter. When the Torah states that God created the heaven and earth, it means that He created, in potential, all spiritual entities and worlds as well as all physical matter.

This idea is mirrored in the modern description of the big bang, the standard model of the universe, in which science describes the entire physical universe, consisting of billions of galaxies, as having begun from an almost infinitely small point of matter. Within that single point existed all that would ever be created.

Heaven and earth symbolize the dualistic appearance of outer reality, a world of opposites and paradox. The ladder represents not just a unifying force between opposites, but also the actual mission of the Jewish people. This idea will be developed in greater detail in a later chapter.

The Sages teach that the ladder and the angels allude to the giving of the Torah at Sinai, due to the fact that the numerical value of the word *sulam*, ladder, equals 130, the same as the numerical value of *Sinai* (*Bereishit Rabbah* 68:16). The ladder being set firmly in the earth alludes to the Jewish people standing at the foot of Mount Sinai on the day the Torah was given; the head of the ladder reaching heaven hints to the verse, "And the mountain burned with fire until the heart of heaven" (Deuteronomy 4:11). The angels ascending and descending allude to Moses and Aaron, who ascended and descended many times in the days leading up to the giving of the Torah; God appearing at the top of the ladder hints to the verse, "And God descended on Mount Sinai, on the top of the mountain" (Exodus 19:20).

"The actions of the fathers are a sign for their children" (*Sotah* 34a). This important statement teaches that not only do subsequent generations learn from the deeds and values of our patriarchs and matriarchs, but also that the patriarchs and matriarchs paved the way for all future generations through their thoughts, speech, and actions. Even deeper, the power and intent of their deeds are engraved in the very essence of future Jewish souls. God revealed to Jacob in the dream the future history and the mission of the Jewish people, as well as profound instruction on their unique spiritual path.

We are also taught that the ladder and angels relate to the service of the priests, the *kohanim*, in the Tabernacle and Temple (*Bereishit Rabbah* 68:16). The ladder set in the earth symbolizes the altar, which was made of earth; the ladder itself represents the ramp leading to the top of the altar. The head of the ladder symbolizes the sacrifices whose smoke reached heaven; the angels ascending and descending represent the *kohanim* ascending and descending on the ramp.

Although we no longer have a Temple, the Temple service serves as a model of how to serve God in all generations. After the Temple's destruction, the Sages translated the Temple service into a new type of service to take place in the synagogue. The prayers and rituals we observe today mirror the very service shown to Jacob in his dream.

The ladder set firmly in the earth with its head reaching the heavens suggests a holistic attitude towards life and an important lesson on how to orient oneself in the world. Our feet must be on the earth, firmly grounded in the realities of the world, yet at the same time our head must be in the heavens, striving to ascend to ever higher levels of spirituality. Most people have a very difficult time balancing these two aspects of life. The tendency is to become entrenched in the material world, entangled by the demands of economic pressure and the need to keep up appearances. Alternatively, some have a tendency to live in a fantasy world, disassociated from practical reality, ruled by fleeting fantasies of either a spiritual or physical nature.

Neither of these approaches is healthy. The Jewish way is to balance the realities of the physical world with regular injections of spiritu ality. Even more than a balancing act, the ladder represents a unique worldview where one actually ascends to higher levels of spirituality specifically by involvement in the physical world. Not only does a Jew infuse the physical word with holiness, but also rectifying the physical world becomes a catapult to reaching higher spiritual planes.

The ladder also symbolizes the faith and knowledge that no matter where one finds himself on the ladder of life, God is ever present. King David, who, like Jacob, lived a turbulent life of highs and lows, expressed it in the following way: "Where could I go from Your spirit or where could I flee from Your presence? If I would ascend to heaven, You are there; and if I were to make my bed in the lowest hell, You are there. If I were to take the wings of dawn and dwell in the distant west, even there Your hand would lead me and Your right hand would hold me" (Psalms 139:7–9). There is no place devoid of God's love and support. For Jacob, who was traveling alone into the unknown, this was an immediate and important message.

In *Netivot Shalom*, the Slonimer Rebbe teaches that a Jew needs to be involved in the physical world and in the service of God (*Netivot Shalom, Parashat Vayeitzei*). The ladder represents the path of Torah, which is broad enough to include both types of activities. He quotes the Midrash, which teaches that some time before this dream Jacob saw the whole world in front of him like a wall (*Bereishit Rabbah* 68:12). After an entire life secluded in the tents of Torah, explains the Slonimer Rebbe, going out into the world seemed like a high wall, impossible to scale. God showed him that the earth and the heavens were not exclusive realms; rather, they are intrinsically connected and one can maintain a life of Torah and holiness wherever one finds himself. The most important thing is to stay on the ladder and within the framework of holiness no matter how the wind blows.

A teaching of the Baal Shem Tov reveals an additional angle to the above teaching. The Baal Shem Tov taught that the numerical value of the word *sulam*, when it is spelled with a *vav* (סולם), is 136, the same as the numerical value of *mamon*, money. Money has the power to drive people to the ground, revealing their most egotistical drives and instincts, yet it can also be used to help others and accomplish great spiritual things. Money is by nature neutral. Its ultimate worth is dependent on what man does with it.

Another word with the value of 136, the equivalent of *sulam*, is *kol*, "voice." When Jacob stood before his father disguised as his brother Esau, Isaac remarked: "The voice is the voice of Jacob, and the hands are the hands of Esau" (Genesis 27:22). Esau represents the physical, material world, while Jacob represents the spiritual world. This dichotomy is exactly what the symbol of the ladder was to teach Jacob — that his mission was to combine both worlds while staying within the holy framework of the ladder. This was actually Rebecca's intent in insisting that Jacob receive the blessing from Isaac — that Jacob toil in both worlds, ultimately bringing them into harmony and balance.

The voice of Jacob also alludes to prayer. The ladder, in a sense, was a physical image in dream form of his prayer before retiring that auspicious night. We have learned that even prophetic dreams can be hidden in the dreamer's own thoughts and inner conflicts. In a later chapter we will analyze Jacob's dream according to our multilevel ladder of dreams, but suffice it to say here that the symbol of the ladder and the angels in many ways are a result of Jacob's own deliberations, struggles, and prayers, the essential context of the dream.

It is interesting to note that during the *mussaf* (additional) prayer on Rosh HaShanah and Yom Kippur we recite, "U'*teshuvah, u'tefillah, u'tzedakah ma'avirin et ro'a hagezeirah* — Repentance, prayer, and charity cancel a harsh judgment!" Above the three words *teshuvah, tefillah,* and *tzedakah* appear three other words in smaller print: Above "*teshuvah*" is the word "*tzom,*" fasting; above "*tefillah*" is the word "*kol,*" voice, and above "*tzedakah*" is the word "*mamon,*" money. We have just discussed the words *mamon* and *kol,* and earlier we discussed the custom to fast for a negative dream. All three of these words share the same numerical value — 136 — the same as *sulam,* ladder! Each of these activities cancels harsh judgment and serves as a special conduit, a virtual ladder, from man to God.

# The Ladder and the Hebrew Letters

We have seen how analyzing a word according to its component Hebrew letters yields deep insight into the essence of the word. The word סולם, ladder, interestingly has three of the same letters as חלום, dream. This alone points to Jacob's dream of the ladder as being perhaps the quintessential and most universal of all Biblical dreams.

As we discussed above in relation to *chalom*, the *lamed* relates to the aspiration of the heart, a sense of climbing, the desire to learn, and the concept of cycles. The ladder in Jacob's dream most certainly relates to the aspirations of his heart and to a sense of climbing to the very heavens. God used the dream to teach Jacob and all subsequent generations a host of life's lessons. Finally, the angels ascending and descending represent in graphic terms the idea of cycles.

The form of the *vav*, that of a man standing erect on the ground with his head in the heavens, is the exact idea symbolized by the ladder. The *vav* is a hook, and its function is to connect, just like the ladder in the dream.

The *mem*, the final letter of both words, represents transition from one state of reality to another. At the time of the dream, Jacob was in a state of transition between Israel and the Diaspora, between singlehood and marriage, between immersion in Torah and involvement in the world.

Finally, the first letter of *sulam* is *samech*, ס, whose form is a circle. The letter *samech* means "to support," and its numerical value is sixty. Similar to the final *mem*, the circle of the *samech* also connotes cycles. Even more than the *mem* and *lamed*, which connote cycles because of their numerical values, the actual circular shape of the *samech* is a universal symbol for cycles. A circle surrounds, and therefore the initial letter of the Hebrew word "to surround," *sovev*, is a *samech*. It could be understood that God, appearing from above, was manifesting Himself to Jacob in His transcendent aspect of *Sovev Kol Olamin*, the One who surrounds all worlds.

Another aspect of cycles in relation to the dream is the revelation Jacob received regarding the unfolding of Jewish history through cycles of exile and redemption, as will be explained below.

*Samech* means to support, an idea clearly seen in the words God speaks to Jacob in the dream: "Behold, I am with you; I will guard you wherever you will go, and I will return you to this land, for I will not forsake you until I have done what I have spoken about you" (Genesis 28:15). God goes out of His way, so to speak, to lend support to Jacob in his precarious position.

The circle also represents the wedding ring in Jewish ritual. This can be understood on two levels: first, as relating to Jacob, who was journeying in order to get married, and second, more allegorically, as relating to the relationship between God and the Jewish people. We have mentioned above the Sages' interpretation of the dream as an allusion to Mount Sinai and the receiving of the Torah, which is described throughout the mystical tradition as the "marriage" between God and the Jewish people. The ladder also represents the natural give-and-take ebb and flow between husband and wife.

The numerical value of *samech* is sixty. We have seen this number in the two statements that sleep is one-sixtieth of death and dreams are one-sixtieth of prophecy. In Jewish law the ratio of one-sixtieth is the amount of a substance that can be considered null and void within another substance. Both sleep and dreaming entail a level of nullification. During sleep the soul leaves the body, thus its comparison to death, while dreaming occurs when the intellect is nullified by the power of imagination and the subconscious.

The ladder in Jacob's dream is a simple image, but as a classic archetypal symbol it connects all worlds and serves as a paradigm for life itself.

# The Angels

Behold, the angels of God were ascending and descending on it.

(Genesis 28:12)

The language of this verse, at first glance, seems quite puzzling. It would seem more logical for angels, who are spiritual beings, residing in the upper worlds, to first descend and then ascend. Rashi explains that the angels of the Land of Israel, who had been accompanying Jacob until that point, were the ones ascending, while a different band of angels, who would accompany him outside the land, descended to greet him. When Jacob returns to the Land of Israel twenty years later, the very opposite occurs: "Jacob went on his way [towards the Land of Israel] and angels of God encountered him. And Jacob said when he saw them, 'This is a Godly camp.' And he called the name of the place Mahanaim" (Genesis 32:3). The word *Mahanaim* means "camps," in the plural, and Rashi explains that Jacob saw the angels of outside the land and the ones of the Land of Israel trading places once again.

The idea of variant bands of angels for different geographical places can be associated with a few other ideas as well. On Shabbat eve, as we gather around the table for the first meal of Shabbat, the song "*Shalom Aleichem*" is sung. The first stanza of this song welcomes angels of peace, who hover around the Shabbat table in this special moment of holiness. The second stanza invites them to come closer, the third requests that they bless us, and the fourth sends them away in peace. The question is asked, Why are we sending the angels away so soon — didn't we just greet them? One possible answer is that there are actually angels for the week and angels for the Shabbat, just as there are angels for Israel and other angels for outside of Israel. When we greet the angels at the beginning of *Shalom Aleichem* we are greeting the angels of Shabbat, while at the end of the song we are bidding farewell to the angels of the six days of the week. In other words, every Shabbat there is a changing of the guard, for the angels of Shabbat are on a higher spiritual level than the angels of the week.

Another application of this idea is at a Jewish wedding. The groom and bride are accompanied to the wedding canopy individually, by their parents, in a special and solemn atmosphere. After the ceremony, groom and bride are accompanied away from the canopy by throngs of singing and dancing friends and relatives. This change can also be thought of as a changing of the guard. Groom and bride are led to the canopy as single people, yet when they leave they are married, beginning an entirely new stage of life. Each status requires a different accompaniment, a different group of "guards."

The concept of guardian angels appears in the Midrash, which states that Jacob saw the guardian angels of the four different nations that would rule the Jewish nation in their various exiles. First he saw the protective angel of Babylonia ascend seventy rungs and then fall, a sign that the Babylonian exile would last seventy years. Next, the angel of Persia and Media climbed fifty-two rungs, only to fall as well. This was a sign that the Persian-Median exile would last fifty-two years. The guardian angel of Greece then ascended 120 rungs and he too descended. Finally, the angel of Rome began to climb. It rose higher and higher with no end in sight. (Rome is the present exile, which has lasted nearly two thousand years.) Jacob grew very fearful and asked God if the last exile would ever end. God assured him that He Himself would bring the angel down in due time (*Vayikra Rabbah* 29:2).

Along with this ongoing cycle of exile and redemption in Jewish history, Jacob was shown the giving of the Torah on Mount Sinai and the Temples and their destruction (*Bereishit Rabbah* 69:6).

Another explanation of why the angels were ascending and then descending relates to the relationship between Jacob and Esau, from whom Rome descends. Jacob and Esau were twins and shared a classic love-hate relationship, whose energy has been manifest throughout the generations. According to Jewish tradition, Rome comes from Esau and from Rome came the institutionalized Christian church. We can now better understand the prophecy received by Rebecca: "Two nations are in your womb; two peoples from your insides will be separated. One people shall be stronger than the other, and the elder shall serve the younger." The Roman conquest of Israel and the subsequent tortured relations between Judaism and Christianity demonstrate how very true this prophecy was.

An interesting dynamic is revealed in the words, "and the one people will be stronger than the other." The Sages teach that when one nation is strong and on the ascent, the other will fall; they will never be equally strong (*Megillah* 6a). This is seen clearly, for example, in the story of Purim, where Haman (a descendant of Esau) and Mordecai (a descendant of Jacob) take turns in ascendancy. Upon hearing that the tide had begun to turn against Haman, Zeresh, his wife tells him, "If Mordecai before whom you have begun to fall is of the seed of the Jews, then you will not prevail against him, but you will surely fall before him" (Esther 6:13).

The angels' ascension and descension revealed to Jacob multilayers of meaning: from his own tortured relationship with his brother to the entire picture of Jewish history.

# In the Service of God

Just as the ladder in Jacob's dream contains many allusions to spiritual striving, so too does the image of the angels ascending and descending on it. The angels first ascending and then descending hint at the ideal way of drawing close to God, referred to in Kabbalah and Chassidut as "an arousal from below." This occurs when a person on his own initiative arouses himself to draw closer to God. However, in the times when we run out of steam, falling into complacency and boredom or, worse, into depression and a sense of futility, the arousal must come "from above," from God. The angels first ascending from below teach us the ideal way to approach God. When we lack the inspiration to motivate ourselves from below, it behooves us to pray to God to assist us by arousing us, at least initially, from above. God, in His great mercy, may not wait for us to make the first move, but rather will send us an unmistakable sign or message from above that moves us towards a new awareness. This is hinted at by the descending angels.

The idea of angels ascending initially from below symbolizes another remarkable concept in Jewish tradition, especially in Kabbalah and Chassidut: that human thought and action actually create angels.

Angels are spiritual energy forces existing in all the created worlds. They help direct different aspects of creation and are also intrinsically bound up with the material world, as the Sages teach: "No blade of grass grows until its [guiding] angel above strikes it and says, 'Grow' " (*Bereishit Rabbah* 10:7). In addition to each individual detail of creation having a guiding spiritual force, all the species and orders of creation have a corresponding spiritual force above, their animating root force, guiding and sustaining their development in this world. There exists an incredibly complex hierarchy of these spiritual energy forces, called angels, in all the various worlds. Each human being and nation as well has its protective angel. These were the angels that Jacob saw in his vision of the enfolding of Jewish history, discussed above.

According to Jewish tradition, the source of the human soul is rooted in a higher world than the source of angels. This is because angels do not possess free will, a crucial component of spiritual advancement. Free will is perhaps the most important qualification of being in the "image of God."

Along with angels who direct and perform their tasks as loyal agents of God from above, there is another class of angels created through the actions of man below. Just as no action below occurs without a corresponding action above, so too, no action below occurs without creating energy which then affects the upper worlds. The Sages therefore taught that man's actions create angels, energy forces who, according to the moral and ethical value of the action, become either defending angels or prosecuting angels. It was in this light that Rabbi Eliezer ben Yaakov said: "He who fulfills even a single mitzvah gains himself a single advocate, and he who commits even a single sin gains himself a single accuser…" (*Avot* 4:13).

We are affected by spiritual forces from above, yet perhaps more profoundly, we affect the essential fabric of all the spiritual worlds from below. The intrinsic link existing between the physical and spiritual worlds creates a complex web of interactions and mutual influence.

As Jacob lay and dreamt that awesome night, he was creating angels as well as receiving Divine instruction through "angels of God." All this was occurring on a multitude of levels simultaneously. His dream was a projection from below of his hopes and fears, his thoughts and his anxieties, as he strode into the future. From above, God was sending messages of comfort and revelation. This all translated into angels ascending and descending on a ladder firmly set in the earth with its head reaching the heavens.

# God and the Head of the Ladder

And behold God was standing over him, and He said, "I am God, God of your father Abraham and God of Isaac. The ground upon which you are lying I will give to you and to your descendants…."

(Genesis 28:13)

When God appeared to Jacob he was "standing over him"; in the aspect of *Sovev Kol Olamin*, surrounding and transcending all worlds, symbolized by the letter *samech*, the first letter of *sulam*, ladder. Yet when He speaks to Jacob it is the revelation of not just God's transcendent being, but His aspect of *Malei Kol Olamin*, filling all worlds, as well. This is one of the paradoxical mysteries of God — that He is beyond all concept of time and space, yet at the same time is ever present in every moment and place.

The body of man, like that of an animal, is designed for survival and physical pleasure. The soul, on the other hand, longs to know and unite with God. The body is like water, which seeks to fall to the lowest plane, while the soul is like fire, flaming passionately upwards. This dual dynamic is also alluded to in the movements of the angels on the ladder.

God at the head of the ladder represents the source and the purpose of all existence. He both hovers above all creation and is intimately involved in all that transpires. The soul's longing to climb higher and higher until it reunites with God is also paradoxical, for finite man can never truly reach that goal. Nonetheless, the soul is undeterred. No matter how many times it descends, its natural, instinctive impulse is to try ascending once again.

The only way to experience even the hint of union with the Divine is through self-nullification. This too is paradoxical, as the only way to truly unite with God is by nullifying, in a sense, one's very existence. The soul intuits on a very primordial level that its existence is bound up in the very essence of God.

God's words to Jacob in the dream, which is the first instance recorded in the Torah of God speaking to Jacob, reaffirm the covenant that God made with Abraham and Isaac. God is not only showing support for Jacob in his journeys, but is also appointing him as the third of the patriarchs. In fact, God's promise to give Jacob and his descendants the land he is lying on mirrors the very first covenant God made with Abraham, also a covenant of the land.

The fact that only God — and not the angels — speaks to Jacob in the dream points to another important concept. The Talmud states that unlike other nations who are under the influence of the stars and have a guiding angel directing and overseeing their welfare, Israel is not ruled by the stars, but rather is under the direct providence of God (*Shabbat* 156a). Although Jacob, as a symbol of all Israel, is touched and influenced by angels and all other forces of nature, ultimately his direct link is to God, and God alone.

In truth, we have just scratched the surface of the profound symbolism of Jacob's dream. The more one probes into any part of the Torah, the greater the hidden treasures one discovers. In upcoming chapters we will continue to expand on many of the themes introduced in this chapter as we attempt to translate the symbols of Jacob's dream into relevant and timely teachings for us today. Before continuing our analysis of the symbolism of the ladder, though, we will first try to understand some of the deeper concepts contained in Jacob's reaction to the dream and then explore the mystery of the place of the dream.

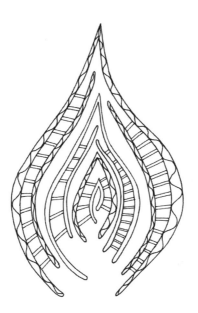

# 10

# Jacob's Reaction to the Dream

h en Jacob awoke from his sleep, he said: "Surely God is in this place, and I did not know!" (Genesis 28:16). His response was very different than that of Pharaoh, who also awoke suddenly from his dream but quickly fell back asleep (ibid. 41:4–5). Jacob was immediately aware of the awesomeness of the dream. Yet his reaction was not "God *was* in this place," but "God *is* in this place." In other words, he recognized that his dream and reality were actually one and the same. His dream was not merely a fleeting vision, but God's promise to be with him was quite real.

> And he became frightened and said, "How awesome is this place! This is none other than the house of God, and this is the gate of heavens!"
>
> (Genesis 28:17)

In this verse Jacob reacts with fear to the awesomeness of the place. Fear of God is an indispensable part of our relationship to God, yet the idea often disturbs the sensibilities of Western man. Love of God is somehow easier to relate to. As a result, many choose to translate the Hebrew word for fear, *yirah*, as "awe" instead. This interpretation is supported by this verse, as Jacob's fear is indeed a result of his awe.

Rashi explains that Jacob was now aware that the place where he stood, the future Temple Mount, was the channel through which all prayers ascend, the "gate to heaven." Rashi continues by quoting the tradition that the heavenly Temple is situated directly above the earthly Temple in Jerusalem. This is a further revelation of the symbolism of the dream, which fits well with our previous discussion of the impact that man's actions below have on the upper worlds.

Today, the Western Wall is the last vestige of the Second Temple in Jerusalem. In truth, the Wall is one of the retaining walls of the Temple Mount, not an actual part of the Temple. However, since it is situated right below the place where both holy Temples stood, people from all over the world go there to pray. For thousands of years Jews have directed their prayers to this place, considered to be the gate to Heaven. It is explained that prayers from all over the world travel to the place of the Temple and ascend to Heaven from there. In this sense the Temple acts as an inverted pyramid, a vortex of prayer and energy streaming upward while Divine bounty and influx flow downwards.

Many people experience some sort of spirutal uplifting when they visit the Wall. A person who is sensitive enough can feel not only all the prayers being directed to the Western Wall in the present, but even all the prayers of the past which have left their impression on the place. With great arousal one can even feel the Temple of the future and the atmosphere of joy and peace that will one day emanate to the whole world from the third and eternal Temple. Praying at the Western Wall is like plugging into a timeless grid of energy. It is no wonder that its effects are so spiritual and mystical.

> Jacob arose in the morning and he took the stone that he had placed around his head and set it up as a pillar, and he poured oil on its top.

> (Genesis 28:18)

Jacob immediately acted upon his dream, consecrating the stone. This is an additional sign that he interpreted the dream as something he needed to act upon and integrate into his being.

As we discussed above, this stone is in fact the twelve stones which Jacob originally placed around his head. God fused the stones together and this became an integral part of His revelation to Jacob. These twelve stones becoming one can also indicate Jacob's own ability to integrate the meaning of the dream until it became one with his consciousness.

The one stone further symbolizes Jacob's understanding that the oneness of God is essentially bound up with the oneness of Israel. This idea is expressed in the afternoon prayer on Shabbat: "You [God] are one, and Your name is one, and who is like Your people Israel, one nation in the earth?" The tefillin, phylacteries, of a Jew, contain the cardinal statement of Jewish faith: "Hear, Israel, God is our God, God is one [unique]." We are taught in the Talmud that God "wears" tefillin as well, as it were. What verses do God's tefillin contain? The Talmud teaches that they contain the above quote: "You are one and Your name is one, and who is like Your people Israel, one nation in the earth?" (*Berachot* 6a). The mission of the Jewish people is to reveal God's oneness in the world; God takes pride, as it were, in the Jewish people and their national and individual striving to fulfill their chosen mission.

Another subtle, yet beautiful, allusion to Jacob's ability to interpret the symbols in his dream and apply them to his life is learned from the words used to describe him setting up the stone as a pillar. The word for "pillar," *matzeivah*, is from the same root as the word "*mutzav*," used to describe the ladder being set firmly in the earth. Jacob poured oil on the top ("*rosh*") of the pillar, the same word used for the head of the ladder. His act of anointing the pillar is a transformation of the symbols of the ladder into reality.

Jacob named the place Beit-El, which means "the house of God" (Genesis 28:19). The Talmud teaches that each of the patriarchs described Mount Moriah in a different way (*Pesachim* 88a). Abraham called it a mountain, after the awesome events surrounding the binding of

Isaac: "And Abraham called the name of the place 'Hashem Yireh,' as it is said to this day, on the mountain God will be seen" (Genesis 22:14). Isaac called it a field, as it is written: "And Isaac went out to converse [with God] in the field towards evening" (ibid. 24:63). Jacob called it a house, as we read above: "...This is none other than the house of God...."

The progression from mountain to field to house represents a process of internalizing and personalizing our human relationship with God. After the dream, Jacob took an oath that if God protected him along his way as He had promised and returned him to his father's house, "then this stone which I have set up as a pillar will become a house to God, and whatever You give me I shall surely give a tenth to You" (Genesis 28:20–22). For Jacob, this place must be more than a setting where man and God meet "outside"; it must be transformed to a dwelling place where man and God meet on the "inside."

The Tabernacle in the desert represented this "inside" relationship, where God would dwell in the midst of the Jewish people. Yet the Tabernacle's transitory nature indicated that a fuller manifestation was still called for. The complete progression was not fully manifest until King David conquered Jerusalem and envisioned a permanent dwelling place for God on earth. Although it is clear that God is in all places and at all times, nevertheless, the Temple, built by David's son Solomon, symbolizes man's creating a true home for God, not only as revealed in a physical building, but also, more importantly, in man's own heart and mind.

Jacob's promise to tithe whatever God gives him is connected to the numerical value of *sulam* being 136, the same as that of *mamon*, money. Jacob once again transformed the lessons of the dream in an immediate and practical manner.

After Jacob sets up his pillar, the Torah states: "And Jacob lifted up his feet and went towards the land of the people of the east" (Genesis 29:1). Here we see Jacob acting with enthusiasm, as symbolized by his lifting up his feet. This is another indication that Jacob integrated the dream until it permeated his entire being — from his head to his toes.

His traveling to the land of the east is highly symbolic in a number of ways. Abraham left Ur Kasdim, in the land of the east, in order to spread the teachings of the One God. Jacob was returning there to begin the long process of rectifying the world, the quintessential mission of the Jewish people. His lifting his feet symbolizes his intent to lift up the material world to its spiritual source.

The Hebrew word for east is *kedem*, the same root as *Adam Kadmon*, the name of the highest of spiritual worlds, as discussed previously. The root *kedem* means "previous" or "primordial." Rectification depends on transformation occurring in essence and at the source, so that change is permanent and complete. As Jacob began his journey with newfound hope and excitement, he understood that he would need to dig deep within his own essence to extract the strength he needed to accomplish his mission.

This looking inward is reflected in the very next verse: "He looked and behold — a well in the field" (Genesis 29:2). The word *behold*, which is used throughout the dream, is now part of Jacob's life and perspective. The well is symbolic of Jacob beginning to draw into reality his own unique living waters, as his fathers and mothers had before him.

# 11

# The Place

fter setting up his pillar and anointing it with oil, Jacob proceeded to name the site of his dream. The verse states:

And he called the name of the place Beit-El, although Luz had been the city's name originally.

(Genesis 28:19)

This is quite puzzling, since, as we discussed above, the Sages in the Midrash teach that Jacob's dream took place on the Temple Mount in Jerusalem (see *Rashi* on Genesis 28:11). Upon close inspection, we see that the word "place" appears six times in the incident of the dream of Jacob. Due to a certain measure of vagueness in the text, there is much discussion among the Sages as to where the place actually was.

In a long and involved commentary on verse 17, Rashi quotes the opinion of Rabbi Yosei that the foot of the ladder was in Beersheba (to the south) and its head was in Beit-El (to the north), while the middle of its slope was above the Temple Mount. Rashi then develops another idea, based on the teaching in the Talmud that the Temple Mount "came towards Jacob" or that the "ground shrank." In an alternative explanation of "he came upon the place" — which Rashi had previously interpreted as Jacob having prayed there — he explains that Jacob "met the place as two people who are moving towards each other meet." (See in total the *Rashi* on Genesis 28:17).

To add to the mystery are Rashi's comments on the promise of God that "the ground upon which you are lying, I will give to you and to your descendants" (Genesis 28:13). Taken literally this could be understood that God was promising the land Jacob was lying upon, and no more! However, Rashi quotes the opinion of the Talmud that God "folded up the entire Land of Israel under him, thereby hinting to him that it would be as easily conquered by his descendents as a piece of land four cubits in length, the space covered by a person lying down" (*Rashi* on Genesis 28:13; *Chullin* 91a).

It is clear from these comments by Rashi that great secrets regarding the nature of space are to be found here. We hope to discuss below various ways to understand what the Talmud and Rashi are alluding to in these enigmatic references to "the place."

# Folding Up Space

We discussed earlier how time is not truly a constant (see chapter 5, "Dreams and the Mystery of Time"). Both science and subjective experience confirm this. We also saw how time can expand and contract nearly without limit in dreams. We touched briefly on how these same ideas apply to space as well. Rebbe Nachman taught that the greater the intellect, the less both time and space are strictly defined and limited in application.

Rabbi Yitzchak Ginsburgh teaches that all of time is contained in potential in every moment of time and all of space is contained in potential in every point of space. We have already given some examples regarding time. Let us now concentrate on seeing how each point of space contains all space in potential.

Perhaps the best example of this is the scientific explanation of the origins of the universe. According to the standard model of the universe, popularly known as the "big bang," the present universe of billions of galaxies all began from an almost infinitely small point of matter. This is truly a startling idea, yet it concords with our statement that all that exists today and will ever exist in the material universe was once contained in a single point.

This reality is actually repeated throughout nature. Every plant and animal, as well as every human being, begin as a seed. In fact, the entire DNA code is replicated in virtually every cell of the body. These are all examples of space "folding" in on itself, containing in seed form the entire entity that will later develop from it.

Other examples of Rashi's ideas of space "shrinking" or "coming towards us" are seen in the phenomenal changes that have taken place in all forms of technology and communications in the last century. A journey which once took months can be accomplished today in half a day; what was formerly an all-day trip can be covered in an hour. A letter which would have taken days, weeks, or months to arrive at its destination now takes seconds by fax or e-mail. All these cases, which would have been classified as miraculous just 150 years ago, are now normal and expected. As Rabbi Nachman explained, the greater the intellect, the less space is defined and limited.

The above examples also apply to thoughts and dreams. The Baal Shem Tov taught that a person is where his or her thoughts are. This is true emotionally and in a certain sense spatially as well. For a sick or elderly person, walking ten feet may be impossible to imagine, while for an energetic and healthy person traveling halfway around the globe is no problem at all. In our dreams we can soar above the earth or circle the globe in minutes or seconds. Today's dreams and science fiction fantasies may well be tomorrow's reality.

Where Jacob was physically lying was less important to the Sages than where the dream was really happening. The symbolism and the allusions in the verses all point to Jacob being on the Temple Mount, whether he came to it or it came to him, or perhaps, as Rashi states, they met in the middle.

# The Primordial Contraction

H aving all of the Land of Israel folded up under Jacob alludes to the deep and primordial concept of *tzimtzum*, contraction, as expounded upon by the Arizal, Rabbi Yitzchak Luria. Based on teachings from the *Zohar* and other texts, the Arizal constructed a cosmological model of Creation strikingly similar to the standard model of the universe of modern science. Central to his model was the idea of *tzimtzum*, contraction, in which God, as it were, contracts His infinite being in order to make "a place" for the creation of a finite, material world. In the place where the contraction occurs a vacuum is formed, a "place" in which the world can be created.

Chassidut explains that the contraction is only from a limited human perspective; from God's vantage point no contraction occurred at all. In addition, Chassidut teaches that the vacuum, which would have appeared totally empty from our perspective, contained "an impression" of the original infinite presence of God.

The idea of "shrinking" space or "folded up" space in all the above examples bring us closer to a more Divine perspective on space. Just as God is above time, and from a Divine perspective past, present, and future all occur simultaneously, so too, with regard to space. From a Divine perspective, all space exists within every point of space.

The terms "folded up space," "shrinking space," and the like have startling similarity to modern science's description of time and space. In 1905, Einstein's theory of relativity revealed the elasticity of time and space and how they are stretched, warped, and shrunk, curved, bent and twisted. Gravity is now understood to be the result of the mass of an object "warping" the space around it. A black hole is a place where space-time is so warped that even light entering its gravitational field cannot escape. These ideas of the warping of space-time and how gravity works fit amazingly into Rashi's explanations of our text.

The dynamics of contraction and vacuums exist within the human psyche as well. For new spiritual advancement to occur, we must sometimes experience a psychological and emotional contraction in order to make "space" for spiritual growth. This insight sheds light on Jacob's state of mind as he "came upon the place." The word *place* appears three times in the sentence preceding his dream, an indication that Jacob was psychologically ripe for a new stage of life, ready to expand and be filled with new light and revelation.

This idea is supported beautifully by the message of the dream. God first promises Jacob the land he is lying on, which symbolizes the concept of *tzimtzum*. Then, in the very next verse God promises that his descendants will spread out in all directions, symbolizing expansion.

All of Israel being "folded up" under Jacob hints to the very nature of the Land of Israel. Just as the Jewish people are the smallest nation among the nations of the world (Deuteronomy 7:7), the Land of Israel is but a small dot on the map of the world. Yet we are taught that when the Messiah comes the holiness of the land will expand to all the world. Not only will the holiness of Israel expand to the entire world, but also the holiness of the Holy of Holies in the Temple will expand to all the Temple, the holiness of the Temple will expand to all of Jerusalem, and the holiness of Jerusalem will spread out to all of Israel. Taking this idea one step further, we can understand this to mean that until that day the holiness of the land is mysteriously "folded up" within the small borders of the land.

According to tradition, there were ten ongoing miracles that occurred in the Temple (*Avot* 5:7). Many of the miracles reveal the Temple as a place that defied the laws of nature, including those of space. On Yom Kippur, for example, the Temple courtyard was packed to capacity, yet when the high priest would enunciate the Ineffable Name of God and the people would fall to the ground in awe, there was miraculously enough space for everyone to bow down. Despite throngs of people ascending to Jerusalem for the three annual pilgrimage festivals, no person ever lacked a place to sleep, no matter how crowded the city was.

Another miraculous occurrence in the Temple relates to the Holy of Holies which housed the ark, containing the tablets of the law. According to the Sages, the Holy of Holies was not big enough for the ark to actually fit inside it, but there was a space warp of sorts and it fit in miraculously.

The various descriptions of the miracles of the Temple read almost like a quantum physics primer of today. The language is different, but the reality it explains are the same.

# God and the Secret of the Place

Jacob awoke from his sleep and said, "Surely God is in this place, and I did not know!"

(Genesis 28:16)

Rashi comments that had Jacob known that God was present he certainly would not have slept in such a holy place. Perhaps a deeper reading of the text is that Jacob was expressing a new understanding — that God not only surrounds and animates creation, but is also ever present in space itself. With this awareness Jacob was internalizing a similar insight of Abraham, who built an altar and called to God "*Keil Olam*" (Genesis 21:33), which is usually translated "God of the World." Rabbi Yitzchak Ginsburgh teaches that if the text meant "God of the World" it would have an additional letter *hei* — *Keil HaOlam*. The truer translation is "God [is the] World."

This teaching parallels the Chassidic teaching that when the Torah states that there is none other than God, it means "God is all and all is

God." Unlike a pantheistic view that God is no more than the sum total of the universe, this teaching expresses the belief that there is nothing other than God, and though God surrounds all worlds and is beyond time and space and all description, He is at the same time ever present in every moment of time and every point of space. The following statement perhaps best represents the above paradoxical understanding of God: "He is the place of the world, but the world is not His place" (*Bereishit Rabbah* 68:9).

After the sin of the golden calf, Moses spent forty days on Mount Sinai praying for forgiveness for the nation. As part of the process of forgiveness, God revealed to Moses the Thirteen Principles of Compassion and taught him that no one can see God's face and live. Then God said, "Behold! There is a place with Me; you may stand on the rock. When My glory passes by I shall place you in a cleft of the rock; I will shield you with My hand until I have passed by. Then I will remove My hand and you will see My back, but My face will not be seen" (Exodus 33:21–23). Rashi comments that the text states "There is a place with Me" and not "I am in this place" for God is the place of the world, but the world is not His place.

The "face of God" refers to direct revelation, something beyond the grasp of any finite being. The "back of God" is His hiding in nature, in the reality of time and space. The Arizal taught that all matter, animate or inanimate, large or small, exists due to a spark of God animating it. Jacob, who had spent his entire life cloistered in the tents of Torah, was now encountering the world, as it were, for the first time. God therefore wished to reveal to him that He is truly everywhere, permeating all existence. This revelation is the first step in the process of uniting physical and spiritual, Jacob's life work and mission.

Significantly, one of the names used to refer to God is *hamakom*, "the place." This idea can be seen in a beautiful mathematical gem: when we square each of the four letters of God's name, the total equals 186, the exact numerical value of *makom*, "place"! (The prefex "*ha*" preceding *makom*, meaning "the," indicates that God is the place of the world, but the world is not His place.)

| | | | |
|---|---|---|---|
| 100 = 10 x 10 | 10 = י | 40 = מ |
| 25 = 5 x 5 | 5 = ה | 100 = ק |
| 36 = 6 x 6 | 6 = ו | 6 = ו |
| 25 = 5 x 5 | 5 = ה | 40 = מ |
| 186 = Total of squares | | 186 = Total |

# A Meditation

The six times the word *place* appears in the episode of Jacob's dream can be seen as corresponding to the six directions of a cube, the archetypal form of all space. In his book, *Living in Divine Space* (Jerusalem: Gal Einai, 2003), Rabbi Yitzchak Ginsburgh explains that the six directions of a cube relate to six constant mitzvot incumbent on all Jews at all times and in all places, as taught by Maimonides.

In its introduction, the *Sefer HaChinuch* hints to a further connection between these six mitzvot and the six cities of refuge in ancient Israel, where those who killed inadvertently found haven. Rabbi Ginsburgh teaches that a city of refuge still exists today in a spiritual and psychological sense, in the form of Jewish meditation and specifically in meditating on these six constant mitzvot. Through contemplating the deeper meanings of the mitzvot and their manifold associations with the directions, the *sefirot*, and various archetypal souls that represent these mitzvot and *sefirot*, one orients him- or herself in the middle of the cube, creating a spiritual force field and a true center focus, with which one can then go out into the world.

A person who is meditating represents the middle, seventh point, associated with prayer, a mitzvah which "aspires" to be constant, as taught in the Talmud: "Would that a person pray all the day continually" (*Pesachim* 44b). King David alluded to this when he exclaimed, "I am prayer" (Psalms 109:4).

This meditation, based on the six directions of space, is one of the secrets to shaking the four species in all directions on the holiday of Sukkot.

The seven mitzvot and their related associations are:

| Mitzvah | Direction | Sefirah | Inner Sense | Soul |
|---------|-----------|---------|-------------|------|
| Belief in existence of God | Above | Netzach (victory) | Security | Moses |
| Not believing in other gods | Below | Hod (glory) | Acknowledgment | Aaron |
| Belief that God is One | Front/east | Tiferet (beauty) | Compassion | Jacob |
| Love of God | Right/south | Chesed (kindness) | Love | Abraham |
| Fear/awe of God | Left/north | Gevurah (strength) | Fear | Isaac |
| Not straying after negative thoughts | Behind/west | Yesod (foundation) | Truth | Joseph |
| Prayer | Middle | Malchut (kingdom) | Lowliness | David |

The above chart is the skeleton of the meditation, which is at once powerfully mystical and at the same time very practical in its application to daily life. Once the associations are learned, there is no limit to the depths that can be reached through this and other forms of Jewish meditation.

Meditation in a sense is creating a dream state, where the conscious and subconscious elements of the psyche, the intellect, and the emotions merge together in harmony and creative endeavor. As in a dream, meditation lifts us above the strictures of time and space, allowing the soul to soar to the heart of heaven. Afterwards, one needs to interpret the meditation, just as a dream needs interpreting, in order to fully integrate that which was learned and gained by the experience. The same ideas hold true for visualization, a technique much like meditation used more and more frequently in modern psychology.

If one makes the effort to meditate and contemplate the deep secrets of time and space hidden in the Torah, he will be able to come to the same conclusion as Jacob: "How awesome is this place! This is none other than the house of God, and this is the gate of the heavens!"

## 12

# The Ladder as a Paradigm for Uniting Opposites

e now return to the ladder in Jacob's dream in order to explore in greater depth the meaning of this simple, but powerful, symbol. The ladder is described as being firmly embedded in the earth with its head reaching the heavens, thus connecting these two opposite poles. As we have seen, it is a symbol of connection for many other concepts as well. The ladder has become a paradigm for uniting opposites and teaching us much about the nature of reality and life, as well as about spirituality and spiritual pursuits.

One of the reasons the ladder was shown to Jacob is due to his role in the world. As we have seen, Jacob and Esau represent the conflict between two worldviews. "The youths grew up, and Esau became one who knows hunting, a man of the field, while Jacob was wholesome, a dweller in tents" (Genesis 25:27). Rashi tells us the tents were the tents of learning, while the hunting of Esau was not just for game, but for conniving and tricking his own father.

Esau sold his birthright (and his blessing as well), for his attachment to the material blinded him to the value of the more spiritual birthright. Jacob lived in the world of spirituality, cloistered from the harsher realities of life.

Rebecca saw that ultimately these two worlds must be united, for in essence physicality is not evil in itself; it needs to be uplifted, refined, and channeled properly. Isaac thought Esau and Jacob could find a point of convergence where they would each contribute their portion in the world and that would suffice. Rebecca, however, understood that physical and spiritual, body and soul, heart and mind must be united in a far more internal, essential manner.

The vision of the ladder in the dream was therefore more than a neutral type of symbol for Jacob. It spoke volumes about his personal mission and about the destiny of the Jewish people.

We will now examine a number of seeming opposites and see how the ladder serves as a potent symbol of the unity inherent in them.

# God and Man

God appearing at the top of the ladder while Jacob slept on the earth represents the existential relationship and connection between God and man, the infinite and the finite. The paradox of God and man is encoded in the form of the *alef*, the very first Hebrew letter.

The name of the ideal man is *Adam*, which begins with an *alef*. Many of the most important names of God likewise begin with an *alef*. In his book *The Hebrew Letters*, which this author was privileged to assist in writing, Rabbi Yitzchak Ginsburgh explains the form of the *alef* (א) as a *yud* above, representing God; a *yud* below, representing man; and the letter *vav* representing Torah and mitzvot as the ladder or connecting force between them.

The numerical value of *alef* is one, yet its form paradoxically points to the potential for opposites. One of the meanings of the letter *alef* is a thousand, the symbol of multiplicity and the opposite of unity. The paradox of God and man is the unity and simultaneous separateness that by definition must exist between the infinite and the finite.

Jacob's dream can be viewed in the form of the *alef*: Jacob is the lower *yud*, asleep on the earth; the ladder is the slanted *vav*; and God is the upper *yud*, hovering above.

According to the *Zohar* (3:104b), the *alef* symbolizes more than any other letter the "image of God" in which man was created.

God, as it were, dreams of a dwelling place below, while man dreams to ascend and unite with God above. The ladder, though, reveals an even higher level: man dreaming to bring God down to earth, to infuse physicality with Godliness, to bring a perfected future into a broken present and fully rectify all reality.

The ladder and the angels symbolize the greatest encounter between man and God — the receiving of the Torah at Sinai. We are taught that until that destined meeting God had decreed that higher reality could not totally descend and lower reality could not fully ascend. When the Torah was given God annulled the decree, as it is written: "And God came down to Mount Sinai" (Exodus 19:20), and "Moses approached the cloud..." (ibid. 24:1).

In his dream, Jacob was being shown the paradoxical connection of God and man, and how Torah and mitzvot are the connecting force that bring man Heavenward to God and God, so to speak, down to earth.

# Physical and Spiritual

As we have seen, the greatest personal challenge Jacob faced was uniting the physical realm with the spiritual. In truth, this is everyone's challenge. Nothing appears to be more absolutely opposite than physical and spiritual, yet the ladder in Jacob's dream tells us differently.

The relationship between physical and spiritual can be compared to that of matter and energy. Looking beyond matter's exterior form, we see that it is in essence pure energy. This understanding forever changes our perception of the world we live in. Similarly, when physicality is stripped of its exterior form we find an inner core brimming with spiritual potential. Just as matter and energy are two sides of the same coin, so too, physical and spiritual are intrinsically bonded together.

The name *Jacob*, "Yaakov" in Hebrew, comes from the word *heel*. He was named this because he hung on to the heel of Esau as he was being born. One thing that we can understand from this is that Jacob, representing the spiritual aspect of man, must ultimately manifest his spiritual nature through the physical structure of this world. Even more so, we are taught that, paradoxically, the more the ladder is entrenched in the earth, the higher one climbs towards the heavens. This can only be accomplished, though, if we keep our eye on the ultimate goal of piercing the illusions of physicality in order to extract and uplift the sparks of holiness trapped inside.

The Slonimer Rebbe explains that the process of transforming physical into spiritual is twofold. First we must break all of our attachments to the physical desires and material pulls of this world. Once we are masters of our decision-making process rather than slaves to our base impulses, we can properly use the physical world around us, transforming matter into pure spiritual energy and thus reaching great spiritual heights.

# Body and Soul

E sau represents the body, Jacob the soul. Yet we know that the body needs the soul to survive and the soul needs the body in order to fulfill its mission. The struggle between the body and the soul is not on the theoretical level; it is the basis of our minute-by-minute daily struggles and challenges. As we learned, Adam is a composite of dam, blood, the physical, animal component, and an alef, the Divine soul. The combination of these opposite drives is purposeful on God's part, as it is the perfect arena for the exercising of free will.

The story of the descent of the Jewish people to Egypt is on one level an allegory of the soul descending into the "narrow straits" of the body. The actual meaning of the Hebrew word for Egypt, mitzrayim, is a "narrow place." Coming out of Egypt represents the awakening of the soul, determined to extract itself from the iron grip of the body and to become a free being. The Torah which we received on Sinai is the manual that teaches us how to subjugate the body and train it to work in tandem with the soul. The object is not to devastate or destroy the body but rather to direct and purify it in order to release its hidden potential for holiness. Wandering for forty years in the desert symbolizes the ongoing struggle between body and soul to come to a unity of purpose. Entering the promised land at the end of the journey can be understood as the soul returning to its heavenly abode after its work is finished here below. Alternatively, entering the promised land can symbolize the time of the final redemption when soul and body achieve perfect harmony in this world, a state referred to as the resurrection of the dead.

The lowest level of soul, the nefesh, is most connected to the body and is symbolized by the ladder standing firmly in the earth. The highest level of soul, the yechidah, is the head of the ladder reaching heaven. The ongoing interplay between the body and the various levels of the soul throughout the different stages of life is represented by the angels ascending and descending on the ladder.

# Heart and Mind

I t is said that perhaps the greatest distance in the world is that between heart and mind. Bridging that gap is the work of a lifetime. Yet,
ultimately heart and mind must be aligned and work together to
accomplish our goals in life. In general, we are taught in Chassidut that
the mind must rule the heart, for if not, we are easily swayed by unpre-
dictable mood swings produced by the body and lower aspects of the
soul. Yet the heart, the proverbial seat of the emotions, must not be dis-
missed, as there is a deep level of understanding in the heart that tem-
pers the more calculating coldness of the mind.

The Baal Shem Tov was known to place his hand on the hearts of
Jewish children and bless them to be "warm Jews." The heart is warm, represented by fire; the mind is colder, represented by water. When the letters of the Hebrew word for "the heart," הלב, are permuted, they spell להב,
flame. The initial letter of the Hebrew word for "mind," מח, is a *mem*, the
letter symbolizing water, which begins with a *mem* and ends with a *mem*.

The Hebrew word for ladder is "*sulam*." The *lamed* in this word symbolizes the heart, as discussed above. The last letter of *sulam* is a *mem*,
representing the mind. The angels on the ladder run back and forth between heart and mind, attempting to find a balance that will create a
bridge between earth and heaven.

# Chesed and Gevurah

I n the structure of the *sefirot*, there are three columns — right, left,
and center. C*hesed*, loving kindness, appears on the right side, and
*gevurah*, strength, appears on the left side. According to Kabbalah,

Abraham represents *chesed* and Isaac represents *gevurah*. The two outside pillars are opposites, while the middle column functions as a synthesis between the two. The *sefirot* are arranged in a progression of triangles in order to produce balance and harmony. Jacob, the third patriarch, represents *tiferet*, beauty, the synthesis of *chesed* and *gevurah*.

As Jacob began his journey to forge his own way in the world he was acutely aware of having lived in the shadow of the spiritual giants Abraham and Isaac. Each one represented opposite attributes and natures, each true and tested in its own right. Now Jacob had to find the proper balance and temperament that could integrate both within a new context. In addition to being situated in the center between *chesed* and *gevurah*, *tiferet* is also the middle *sefirah* between above and below, the mind and the heart.

Jacob's dream of the ladder and the angels ascending and descending represented his inner challenge to harmonize all the opposites within the human personality in order to produce a holistic and beautiful rainbow of human achievement.

# Man and Woman

One of the matters certainly on Jacob's mind as he dreamt was his search for a wife. The ladder and the angels are rich with symbolism regarding the relationship between husband and wife, as we will see below.

Despite many attempts in the last half-century to posit that men and women are really the same, the truth is that they are far closer to opposite. Men and women being equal yet opposite is not a value statement but a reality. In fact, this is what makes the attraction between them so strong and creates the equal potential for smooth sailing or stormy seas between the sexes.

A husband and wife must balance the practical, daily needs of a household and family with a more intimate relationship that keeps the fire of love continually burning. The laws of family purity mandate that husband and wife develop, along with their more passionate connection, a relationship that includes intellectual compatibility, emotional stability, and a deep friendship similar to that of a brother and sister. The angels on the ladder allude to the constant give-and-take, ebb and flow of a healthy marital relationship.

Marriage is a fundamental part of Jewish life. We are taught that man and woman cannot fully develop their spiritual natures in isolation or cut off from the physical, and therefore asceticism and celibacy are frowned upon in Judaism.

The *Zohar*, the classic text of Kabbalah, is replete with imagery emphasizing the importance of uniting on all levels the masculine and feminine principles that pervade all reality. In Kabbalah the concept of male and female extends far beyond physical form. It is revealed across the spectrum in the dynamics of opposites that shape all physical and spiritual reality. The relationship of man and woman in marriage is the true testing ground for the unity of so many of the opposites we have discussed till now. As Jacob drew closer to entering into marriage, the symbol of the ladder and the angels had much to teach him, and us as well.

# Israel and the Nations

As we saw in the Midrash, Jacob was given a glimpse of the future history of the Jewish people. The main theme pervading his vision was the ongoing cycle of exile and redemption that would take place over the course of history, molding Israel's relationship with the nations. In particular, we discussed the dynamic between Esau and Jacob, in which when one is in ascendancy the other declines. This is symbolized by the angels ascending and descending.

The relationship between Israel and the nations is very complex and open to much misunderstanding. This is not the proper venue to address such a complicated issue. Nonetheless, the ladder serves as an excellent symbol for the unity between Israel and the nations.

In many ways Israel is unique and set apart from all the nations. On the other hand, there is much that unites Israel with all humanity. Israel is separate and chosen not for the sake of division or isolation, but rather because the ultimate mission of the Jewish people is to bring about true peace and brotherhood among all peoples. This was the constant message and vision of the prophets and is no less true today than it was when they first enunciated their universalistic vision of mankind. In fact, as the hoped-for Messianic era draws closer, the message of world peace and cooperation takes on an even more immediate meaning. One day the entire world will ascend and descend together on the ladder, bringing all mankind close to God and God's kingdom down to earth.

&.&

A symbol is "the little that holds much." The world is full of seeming opposites, and sometimes the distances appear beyond bridging. The ladder is a potent symbol for the hard work that needs to be done and the goals we should be striving for. Yes, like the angels on the ladder we rise and then fall more times than we want to remember. Yet we are taught: "The righteous one falls seven [times] and stands" (Proverb 24:16). The objective of creating unity in all aspects of life lies at the very core of Kabbalistic thought. We may fall, but the goal should never be abandoned. As long as we stay on the ladder, we are going in the right direction.

## 13

# The Ladder and the Secret of Mitzvot

T he usual translation for the word *mitzvah* is "command-ment." While this is certainly correct, we are taught that the root of the word *mitzvah* can also mean "connec-tion" (*Likutei Torah* 2:45c). A mitzvah, like the ladder in Jacob's dream, has the power to connect earth to heaven. A mitzvah is a conduit connecting God and man, and this awareness enriches immeasurably the performance of mitzvot.

This definition is especially important for those who were raised in a secular environment, where the idea of being told what to do runs counter to a superficial understanding of freedom. To most people in the modern world being free means the ability to call the shots, to do whatever one wants. The mere mention of "commandment" may rub a person the wrong way. Understanding a mitzvah as an opportunity to connect to God may strike a more receptive chord.

Performing a mitzvah actually has a connective power on a number of different levels. In this chapter we will construct another five-runged ladder that explains the intrinsic connecting power of a mitzvah. This ladder, similar to the ladder of dreams, is structured according to the five levels of soul. According to the concept of interinclusion, mitzvot are not one dimensional. Rather, their connecting force works simultaneously on multiple levels.

The lowest rung relates to how mitzvot connect us with our bodies and the lowest level of soul, the *nefesh*. The animal soul is essentially bound up with the body. However, its raw energy has great spiritual potential. With ongoing discipline and training through performance of mitzvot, the body and *nefesh* can connect to higher levels of the soul and to God. Over time the body and *nefesh* are refined and directed, resulting in a cooperative effort with the soul. Performing mitzvot demands not just cooperation between body and soul, but also subservience of the basic desires and urges of the body. Yet these desires are not meant to be extinguished; rather, they find full release and expression through mitzvot designed for that very purpose.

Most of the mitzvot include an action, speech, or use of a physical object. In this sense, mitzvot connect our souls not just to our bodies but also to the physical world we live in. The constant interaction with the world through performing mitzvot reinforces the cardinal imperative of Judaism — to rectify, uplift, heal, and transform the world around us.

The next level of soul, the *ruach*, relates to the emotional aspects of the human personality. Mitzvot are not meant to be cold and calculated actions, divorced from the feelings and sensitivities of man. On the contrary, mitzvot bring us into contact with our deeper emotions. We are meant to feel deeply about the mitzvot we do, and the mitzvot are designed to awaken the full gamut of emotions within us, including devotion, love, compassion, awe, and gratefulness. Similar to the *nefesh* which needs constant refining, human emotions are in need of continual tempering and improvement.

The next level of the soul, the *neshamah*, is considered the seat of the intellect. We can involve our *neshamah* in mitzvah performance by seeking meaning and explanations for various mitzvot. The written Torah provides few explanations for the exact meanings of specific mitzvot. It was left to man to study, meditate, and delve into the Torah in order to extract the depths of meaning contained in each mitzvah. Although we ultimately do mitzvot because we are commanded to, we can still use our intellectual powers to unlock the abstract and concrete reasons for and effects of each mitzvah. Learning Torah itself is a mitzvah, one that is considered equal to all the others combined (*Shabbat* 127a). Nothing sharpens, elevates, and clarifies intellect as the study of Torah.

The level of soul termed *chayah*, the "living one," represents the connecting force between the superconscious source of the soul and the beginning of intellectual consciousness. The *chayah* connects the lower levels of soul with their higher Divine origins. At this level, the performance of mitzvot activates and connects the soul to its deepest roots, awakening hidden recesses of spiritual delight and awareness.

The *yechidah*, the highest level of soul, connects us directly to God. At this level we experience a mitzvah as a reflection of God's will and goodness, for all the mitzvot were given with man's good in mind. The last two letters of the word *mitzvah*, ו-ה, are identical to the last two letters of God's essential Four-Letter Name. In one of the Kabbalistic alphabets where letters are exchanged for each other according to a certain logical structure, the first two letters of God's Name, י-ה, are exchanged for the first two letters of the word *mitzvah*. This shows that a mitzvah is ultimately a vessel for God's will and bounty in this finite world. Every mitzvah is ultimately an opportunity to connect to and unite with God.

The angels ascending and descending on the ladder allude to the connective power of mitzvot at all the above levels in the secret of interinclusion. God's will expressed through a mitzvah affects and activates all levels of soul and body within the context of the physical world. In this sense, mitzvot are the quintessential ladder, connecting man and God, physical and spiritual, heart and mind, body and soul, masculine and feminine.

| Level of Soul | Description of Experience | Connecting Force of Mitzvot |
|---|---|---|
| *Nefesh* | Physical | Connecting to the body and the physical world |
| *Ruach* | Emotional | Connecting to the emotions |
| *Neshamah* | Intellectual | Connecting to the intellect |
| *Chayah* | Awareness of God | Connecting to the source of the soul |
| *Yechidah* | Unity with God | Connecting to God |

# 14

# The Ladder of Prayer

I t is written in the *Zohar* that the ladder in Jacob's dream is a metaphor for prayer (*Tikunei Zohar, tikun* 43). This is not hard to understand, based on both the context of the dream and the symbols themselves. As noted above, Jacob prayed when "coming upon the place." His prayer, recited at the beginning of night, became the paradigm for the evening prayer in Jewish tradition. In a sense, the dream was a continuation and superconscious transformation of the content of his prayer.

In the dream, the ladder represents prayer as the connection between man, situated at the bottom of the ladder, and God, who appears at the top of the ladder. The Midrash, quoted above, explained the dream as symbolizing the Temple service: the ladder represented the ramp leading up to the altar, from where the sacrifices rose to God, who appeared above the ladder. The priests who performed the Temple service were represented by the angels ascending and descending on the ladder. After the destruction of the Temple, the Sages transformed the Temple service into the prayer services we practice today.

As noted above, the numerical value of *sulam*, ladder, equals 136, the same as that of *kol*, voice. The ladder is the voice of prayer rising from the heart of man, who is firmly entrenched in the physical world below, till it reaches God, who is ever present above the ladder. Through the act of prayer man's consciousness rises from rung to rung, and his spiritual awareness is elevated to the heights of heaven.

In the accepted rules of Jewish numerology called *gematria*, the numerical value of a word may have the number one added to it in order to reach a certain correspondence. Adding one more to 136 gives us 137, the numerical value of the word *Kabbalah*. In addition to *Kabbalah* meaning "to receive," it also means to make correspondences and proper connections, which Rabbi Yitzchak Ginsburgh teaches is the actual function of Kabbalah. Through learning the inner dimensions of Torah we become sensitized to seeing the incredible web of connections and correspondences throughout all creation. This brings us to a true understanding of the unity and oneness of God.

Based on the teachings of the Arizal, the Baal Shem Tov emphasized the unique opportunity prayer offers to connect directly with God. By reintroducing song and meditation to prayer, he made the experience of prayer into a joyous, and deeply personal experience for the masses. All Chassidic thought and custom follows these teachings of the Baal Shem Tov.

The students of the Baal Shem Tov recorded his various teachings regarding prayer in a treatise called *Amud HaTefillah*, "The Pillar of Prayer." A pillar and a ladder are similar in their function of standing erect and connecting earth to heaven. The name of the quintessential prayer in Judaism is the *Amidah*, meaning standing, from the same root as *amud*, pillar. The ladder being firmly entrenched in the earth represents the humbleness with which a person needs to stand before God, while its head reaching the heavens symbolizes the spiritual potential of man. The emphasis, as indicated by the name of the prayer, is on standing before God, for that is ultimately the stature He envisioned for humanity by creating man "in the image of God."

One of the most important teachings of the Baal Shem Tov, which is included in the above treatise, is his description of three rungs of consciousness which encompass all experience and reality: worlds, souls, and Divinity. That which connects the physical world with the spiritual realms of Divinity is the soul, which, very much like the angels on the ladder, becomes the connecting and unifying force in reality.

At the rung of worlds, man searches for God. At the level of souls, man attempts to serve God. Finally, at the highest rung, man longs to unite with God. In relating to worlds, man's task is to uplift, ascending above the mundane and gravity-bound weight of physicality. Souls are drawn to connect to other souls in intimacy and sharing friendship. The desire of the soul is ultimately to unite with God, losing all sense of individuality.

| Level | Service | Experience |
|-------|---------|------------|
| Worlds | Searching | Uplifting |
| Souls | Serving | Connecting |
| Divinity | Uniting | Uniting |

The three rungs of worlds, souls, and Divinity and the interaction between them describe the constant processing of experience transpiring in our inner consciousness, as well as our daily encounter with reality. They also serve as an accurate description of how our dreams are manifest soul energy going back and forth between multilevels of consciousness, trying to bridge the infinite aspect of God within us and the finite, limited world we live in.

The *Megaleh Amukot* (on Genesis 28:12) states that the ladder in Jacob's dream had four rungs. A great scholar and Kabbalist known as the Shelah correlated the four rungs with the four worlds of Kabbalah (see also *Or HaTorah, Vayeitzei*, vol. 4, p. 838). The Arizal taught that prayer itself should be envisioned as comprising four sections or rungs on a ladder and that these sections relate implicitly to the four ascending worlds of Kabbalah, as we will see below.

The first section of prayer comprises the preliminary morning blessings and Torah verses recited before the prayer "*Baruch She'amar*." This section corresponds to *Asiyah*, the World of Action. We recite the blessings to thank God and acknowledge His goodness in providing us with all our basic necessities, enabling us to function in the world of action. This first section corresponds to the ladder resting upon the earth. We fine-tune our behavioral instincts in order not to take our blessings for granted and strengthen our resolve to use our faculties to the best of our ability.

The second section of prayer is the section referred to as (*Pesukei D'Zimrah*, "Verses of Praise." These prayers comprise a number of the psalms of David, inspiring chapters of praise to God for creating the beautiful world we live in. This section corresponds to *Yetzirah*, the World of Formation. Nature both reveals and hides God. It is for us to search for God and praise His manifest creation, maintaining a sense of awe even when we grow older. This world relates to our emotional attachments and responses to the world around us. Praising God is a positive and constructive way to lift ourselves above the petty emotions and small-minded ego games that at times keep us from even stepping on the ladder of higher ideals and goals in life.

The next section of prayer is arranged around the recitation of the Shema, the cardinal expression of belief in Judaism. This section begins with a description of how the angels daily praise God and leads into the Shema, the ultimate human expression of belief in God. Thus, this section begins with a hint to the angels ascending and descending on the ladder and culminates with man standing humbly before the Creator, ready to speak to Him directly. This once again teaches us that ultimately the soul is rooted in a higher place than even the angels are. This third section corresponds with *Beriyah*, the World of Creation, and relates to the intellect.

It is significant that it is at this level that we express our faith and belief in the oneness of God, for in Judaism belief and faith are ultimately rooted in knowledge and intellect. A beautiful allusion to this idea is found in an acronym formed by the three letters of Adam, *alef*, *dalet*, and *mem*: *emunah*, faith (beginning with *alef*); *da'at*, knowledge (beginning with *dalet*); and *ma'aseh*, action (beginning with *mem*). Our faith, which is based on a deep understanding and knowledge, must be put into practice through actions that reveal and manifest both faith and knowledge.

The final rung on the ladder of prayer is the *Amidah*, the silent prayer. This corresponds to *Atzilut*, the World of Emanation, where man encounters God, who appears above the head of the ladder, in a state of intimate union. Paradoxically, it is at this moment of mystical experience that, along with praise and acknowledgment of God, we communicate to God our private needs and physical requests. This once again emphasizes how ultimately the realms of physical and spiritual, body and soul, heart and mind, temporal and eternal, must be united in a holistic worldview.

| Section of Prayer | Corresponding World | Experience |
|---|---|---|
| Morning Blessings | *Asiyah* (Action) | Thanking |
| *Pesukei D'Zimrah* | *Yetzirah* (Formation) | Praising the works of creation |
| Shema | *Beriyah* (Creation) | Understanding the unity of God |
| *Amidah* | Atzilut (Emanation) | Intimate union with God |

Prayer has many forms and means of expression, both for the individual and for the community. When King David declared, "And I am prayer," he was exclaiming, "Prayer is not something I do — it is who and what I am, it is a state of constant relationship and clinging to God." When Jacob dreamt of a ladder on that auspicious night, he was both consciously and unconsciously acting as a vessel through which prayer was revealed as the means to climb upwards, to stand humbly yet faithfully before God.

## 15

# Five Levels of Understanding the Dream

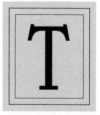hroughout this book we have presented different ideas which correspond to ascending levels of soul and worlds: the ladder of dreams, the ladder of mitzvot, and the ladder of prayer. We now hope to understand Jacob's dream according to the same general organizational scheme.

To review, the five levels of the soul are *nefesh*, the animal soul most connected to the body; *ruach*, relating to the emotions; *neshamah*, corresponding to the intellect; *chayah*, the bridge between the conscious and the superconscious; and *yechidah*, the source of the soul in God.

It must be noted that although we explain Jacob's dream here as emanating in most part from his own inner thoughts, this is but one way to understand a most complex and archetypal dream. By far the most important factor in the dream is the clear communication and revelation of God to Jacob. This was a direct message from God and not a product of Jacob's own thoughts and imagination. We see this clearly in Jacob's own understanding and interpretation of the dream.

Our purpose in explaining the dream according to the various levels of soul and Jacob's inner psychological influences is to show how all the different parts of the soul are interwoven in dreams, as they are in every aspect of life. Sometimes God speaks directly to a person or prophet, as we have seen in a number of Biblical examples, with no intermediating symbolic language or image, but in most cases God speaks to us through the circumstances of our own lives. By understanding on a deeper level the anatomy of the soul, one is able to grasp deeper interpretations of dreams and life itself.

We begin from the immediate bodily influences and the input of the *nefesh*, the lowest level of soul, on Jacob's dream. The need for survival and the desire for pleasure are the hallmarks of the lower animal soul. Yet these two instincts can be clarified and directed for holy purposes.

Jacob arranged stones around his head to protect himself from wild animals, a very basic survival instinct. According to Rashi it was the first time in fourteen years that he had fallen into such a deep sleep. It seems a bit strange that the very night he most feared for his life would be the night he slept the most!

This could indicate that in the process of praying and giving over his fate into the hands of God he actually opened a place within himself to realize how God was, and is, always standing over him, guarding his every step. His initial fear of wild animals — and perhaps his own wild thoughts — forced him to face his most primal fear and work through it until he could actually sleep in confidence and trust.

Rashi states that God caused the sun to go down before its time in order that Jacob should sleep in that place. God was actually acting behind the scenes to arrange things in such a way that His revelation would have the desired effect on every level of Jacob's soul, even the *nefesh*.

On the level of *ruach*, the emotional facet of the psyche, Jacob was wrestling with a host of inner conflicts surrounding leaving his home and his parents, his struggle with Esau, his apprehension about finding a wife and beginning a family. At this, and the previous level of soul, is manifest the opinion in the Talmud that dreams come from a person's own thoughts. In previous chapters we discussed the many levels of symbolism in the dream that relate to these specific inner conflicts. For example, Jacob's vision of the many future exiles related to his own sense of exile; the angels ascending and descending mirrored his own sense of stability or lack of; the angel of Esau rising but not falling accentuated his deepest fear of his brother; and so forth.

The *neshamah*, the intellectual component of consciousness, is active even in a sleep state. Through consciously directing one's thoughts before sleep, or even when asleep, the intellect functions in a more covert, low-key manner, trying at times to solve inner conflicts within a dream itself. Sometimes dreams reveal something that a person knows deep inside but has not yet had the presence of mind or courage to realize. Possible solutions to life's challenges therefore come out in the guise of a dream. Jacob knew that the many levels of symbolism of the ladder and the angels could be seen as his intellect presenting new insight on how to face the obstacles before him.

The level of *chayah* relates to superconscious will in the soul. More than the instinctual will to survive, the soul at this level is connected to its true purpose in life. It is among the greatest gifts of life to become aware of what one's purpose is in this world and then to act according to that deepest calling. The Chassidic expression, "Nothing stands in the way of will," points to the enormous inner potential at each person's disposal.

When Jacob left home he received, along with the blessing he received in Esau's stead, an additional blessing. Isaac, when realizing that Divine providence had caused him to give the blessing to Jacob instead of Esau, blessed him: "And may God bless you, make you fruitful, and make you numerous, and may you be a congregation of peoples. May

He grant you the blessing of Abraham to you and your descendants with you, that you may possess the land of your sojourns which God gave to Abraham" (Genesis 28:3–4). With this blessing, Isaac conferred upon Jacob his destiny and life's work. The symbolism of the ladder and the angels spoke directly to his mission and the spiritual work he and his descendants would undertake. The ladder as a paradigm for uniting opposites especially gave him the tools and the inspiration to go into the world with the intent of bringing light, rectification, and healing.

The highest level of soul is the *yechidah*, the Divine spark within. It is this level of soul more than any other that is a conduit for God's revelation and light. Jacob had spent a lifetime purifying his consciousness, readying himself for God to reveal Himself to him. According to the text, it was in this dream that God first spoke to Jacob. In general, we see that God speaks to those who have made themselves worthy of such revelation.

In truth, it is not only this level of soul that can serve as a channel for God's revelation or message. The will, the intellect, the emotions, and even our most instinctual behavior, when clarified and directed properly, can all act in concert with God's will, as it is written in *Pirkei Avot*: "Treat His will as if it was your will, so that He will treat your will as if it was His will..." (*Avot* 2:4).

This insight is crucial to understanding how at every level of soul Jacob produced the images of his dream, and yet simultaneously God revealed Himself to Jacob in a manner that spoke to all of his deepest conflicts, concerns, and hopes. Just as God caused Jacob to spend the night in such a holy place, He also, in a sense, arranged all of Jacob's life until that moment in order to reveal Himself in this powerful and eternally meaningful fashion. (This insight is also crucial in understanding the mysterious and paradoxical way in which free will and God's providence operate simultaneously.)

The following chart clarifies the ideas presented above.

| Level of Soul | Faculty of Soul | Factor in Dream |
|---|---|---|
| *Nefesh* | Behavioral-instinctual | Fear for survival |
| *Ruach* | Emotional | Inner conflicts based on the past |
| *Neshamah* | Intellectual | Seeking solutions |
| *Chayah* | Superconscious will | Contemplating mission in life |
| *Yechidah* | Spark of God | Direct revelation of God |

Inasmuch as there are seventy faces to the Torah, this interpretation of the inner mechanics of Jacob's dream should be seen as but one of the faces. As we have seen, dreams arise from many different factors and can be interpreted in a myriad of ways. The above interpretation of Jacob's dream, however, is also inherently connected to another event in Jacob's life — the famous incident in which Jacob wrestles with an angel and in so doing receives his name Israel.

This incident took place twenty years later, when Jacob returned to Israel after his years in the house of Laban. He sent a message to Esau that he was returning and received news that Esau was coming to meet him with four hundred men. Jacob grew fearful and did three things to prepare for Esau's coming — he sent gifts to appease him, he prepared for war, and he prayed.

The night before the encounter with Esau, Jacob was left alone. The Torah relates that he fought with a man till dawn. When the man saw he could not defeat Jacob, he injured Jacob in the thigh. He then asked to be sent away, but Jacob refused until he blessed him. At that point, the man conferred the new name of Israel on Jacob: "No longer will your name be called Jacob, but Israel, for you have contended with God and man and have prevailed" (Genesis 32:29). Jacob called the place Peniel, "for I have seen God face to face and my soul has been spared" (Genesis 32:31).

The text and various commentaries offer seemingly contradictory explanations of who Jacob was wrestling with. On one hand it says he was left alone, yet the text mentions a "man." Rashi brings the tradition that it was the angel of Esau. Most significantly, the name *Israel* is defined as "one who fights with God and man," and Jacob himself names the place according to his understanding that he had seen the face of God.

These opinions are in fact not contradictory. Rather, they address different levels of truth and reality all happening simultaneously. The awesome event can be understood to also correspond to the five levels of soul. As in all our previous discussions of interinclusion, here, too, all the various levels interact and affect each other. The somewhat one-dimensional view we present is so much more profound when contemplated deeply.

On the most basic level, Jacob was fighting with himself and his fear of dying by the hand of Esau the next day. This corresponds to the *nefesh*, the lower soul, as he was facing a life-and-death situation. Was he being paranoid and reacting impulsively? Had he reacted correctly by splitting his camp? Should he have run instead? Why was he so afraid, unsure, weak? Surely he wrestled with all these thoughts, produced by his basic instincts, as he prepared for the fateful meeting the next day.

On the emotional level, the *ruach*, the "man" Jacob fought was Esau. All his life Jacob had, in a sense, been holding onto the heel of Esau. He fought with him over the birthright and then over the blessing, and now he would have to fight him again. Jacob knew he must overcome a lifetime of emotional uncertainty and ambiguity to be able to face his brother one more fateful time.

On the intellectual level of the *neshamah*, Jacob understood that his battle with Esau was not just a physical battle but was being fought on a higher spiritual level. For Jacob to defeat Esau physically he would have to defeat him spiritually. On this level Jacob was fighting with the angel of Esau, the higher spiritual force of Esau and what he stood for.

At the level of *chayah*, Jacob was wrestling with his own destiny. His whole life had brought him to this moment when he would have to once and for all vanquish his doubts as to his worthiness and capability of fulfilling his mission in the world. There could be no turning back — he would either be defeated or assume his true identity with no regrets or fear. This explains the great significance of Jacob receiving the name Israel as a result of that incredible, all-night struggle.

At the level of *yechidah* Jacob fought not only with man, but with God Himself. This is seen clearly in the explanation of the name Israel as contending with God and man and prevailing, as well as in Jacob's own perception of who he was struggling with. Jacob's struggle with God epitomizes the struggles of each one of us as we try to understand who we are, why we are here, and how to accept God's providence even when things don't go the way we think they should. Even more it is the struggle to understand how to make God's will our will.

The chart below clarifies these concepts:

| Level of Soul | Faculty of Soul | Struggle |
|---|---|---|
| Nefesh | Behavioral-instinctual | Fear for survival |
| Ruach | Emotional | Internal conflicts with Esau |
| Neshamah | Intellectual | Spiritual roots of conflict with Esau |
| Chayah | Superconscious will | Accepting mission and destiny |
| Yechidah | Spark of God | Understanding relationship with God |

Jacob's struggle that night occurred on all the different levels described above. This timeless event offers incredibly deep insight into the human psyche. In addition, the Jewish people received their name for all time from this event, indicating its long-lasting impact on our mission and destiny.

Although the struggle is not termed a dream in the Torah, it does appear to have occurred in some altered state of consciousness — perhaps a vision or meditation. Yet it was not just a figment of Jacob's imagination, as he was physically injured in the thigh. Perhaps the struggle was happening on a plane of reality that incorporated all levels of soul, making it even more "real" than daytime reality. The enigma of this event exemplifies the mystery of where dreams begin and where reality ends.

# 16

# The Ladder of Life

here is one more paradigm of the ladder which, in a sense, encompasses all we have said till now, and this is understanding the ladder and the angels as symbols of life and existence itself.

A major concept describing the dynamic of all life is termed in Kabbalah and Chassidut "run and return." It is based on a verse in the book of Ezekiel which describes Ezekiel's vision of the chariot, one of the most mystical portions in the Bible: "As for the likeness of the living creatures: their appearance was like coals of fire, burning like the appearance of torches; it spread about among the living creatures; and the fire was hot and from the fire went forth lightning. And the living creatures ran and returned like the appearance of a flash of lightning" (Ezekiel 1:13–14).

The "run and return" of these angels, which Ezekiel termed "living creatures," bears much similarity to the actions of the angels on the ladder in Jacob's dream. The run-and-return dynamic is employed in Kabbalah and Chassidut to describe the pulse of life and existence manifest in countless ways throughout creation: from the contraction and expansion at the very origins of the universe to the pulse of the blood running through our veins; from the cycles of the seasons to the ebb and flow of the tides; from the motion of breath to the beating o

the heart; from the give-and-take of relationships to the cycle of life and death itself.

King Solomon, the wisest of men, expressed it this way in the book of Ecclesiastes: "One generation passes away and another comes, but the earth abides forever. And the sun rises and the sun sets, and it hastens to its place, where it rises again. The wind goes toward the south and then veers to the north; round and round goes the wind, and on its circuits the wind returns. All the rivers run to the sea, yet the sea is not full; to the place where the rivers flow, there they return to flow" (Ecclesiastes 1:4–7).

The ladder symbolizes life itself, while the angels represent the constant dynamic of change and movement. A Chassidic maxim teaches that if one is not ascending on the ladder of life, he is by definition descending, inasmuch as there is no such thing in life as "standing still."

Although angels are used here to represent the run and return of all things, in relation to man they are actually called "standing," as it is written: "If you will walk in My ways and guard My watch…I will give you strides among these who are standing here" (Zechariah 3:7). Angels are called "standing" because they do not possess free will. This is why angels are said to emanate from the World of Formation, whereas the soul emanates from the higher World of Creation.

The Midrash relates (B*emidbar Rabbah* 22:7) that a Roman noblewoman once asked the sage Rabbi Shimon ben Chalafta how long it took God to create the world. He answered, "Six days." She then asked what God has been doing since that time. The sage answered that God is occupied with building ladders in order to elevate some people and at the same time bring others down.

One of the greatest challenges in life is how to contend with the constant run-and-return dynamic, and especially how to balance the highs and the lows of our emotional mood swings. The Baal Shem Tov explained that in the verse "I shall place God before me at all times" (Psalms 16:8), the word for "I shall place," *shiviti*, also means "to make equal." Therefore, he explained the verse to mean: "I will place in my consciousness and accept with equanimity that all that happens to me, at all times, comes from God." In this way of thinking our ups and downs become more relative and easier to handle. However, no matter how much equanimity we accept things with, there is still wisdom in learning to "go with the flow," where we experience the highs and lows but are far less egotistically attached to their permanence.

Achieving peace is a noble concept, but it should not become the end of all Jewish spiritual striving, because in essence peace, in its most idealized notion, is simply impossible to achieve in life on any permanent basis. The name Israel means to contend and to struggle, and that remains our fate and destiny. Yet this is not a negative phenomenon, but rather is an accurate analysis of the realities of life. Of course, this does not minimize the value of experiencing the peace and bliss of Shabbat or finding peace in meditation. These are useful and worthy pursuits, but our destiny is to struggle and achieve and to continually run and return in order to run again.

The Talmud (Berachot 64a) questions whether the righteous will have rest in the World to Come. The answer given is that the righteous will not experience rest in the context of inaction or as a permanent condition, but rather they will ascend from "strength to strength." Even in a future utopian setting there will be constant change and elevation of soul and spirit.

After Jacob returned to Israel, having survived his twenty years with Laban, his encounter with Esau, and a further explosive incident with the city of Shechem, the Torah states that Jacob settled in the land of Canaan (Genesis 37:1). Rashi quotes the Midrash, which teaches that Jacob wanted to settle down to a life of tranquility, but the problems of Joseph came upon him. In the words of the Midrash, God tells those who want to have tranquility in this world: "Is it not enough for the righteous that which is set aside for them in the World to Come? They also want to dwell in tranquility in this world?" This somewhat harsh appraisal is directed at those who think their purpose in life is finished at some defined moment, after which they can dwell in peace. After all he went through, Jacob perhaps thought he had accomplished all that he needed to in this world, and therefore he could now dwell in peace. God was informing him that this was not his fate and he still had what to accomplish.

Of course, finding peace of mind while simultaneously striving for self-improvement and spiritual advancement is not a contradiction, but the best we can truly hope for. On the ladder of life the ups and downs are inevitable, but we have a choice of how to relate to the roller-coaster ride. The choice is not whether we struggle, but which struggles to engage in and how to conduct them.

We might ask at this point how Jacob actually fared after the dream and how much of the symbolism of the dream he was able to integrate and translate into his reality. According to the Sages, Jacob is called the choicest of the patriarchs (*Bereishit Rabbah* 76a), due to his ability to accomplish so much despite constant challenges in the mundane world. He fathered the twelve tribes, establishing them as the foundation of an entire nation. He survived the cunning and deceit of Laban, Esau, and Shechem by fighting them on their own turf and in their own manner. He became materially wealthy, yet maintained his sense of holiness and destiny. His skill in transforming the flocks of Laban into his own reveals his ability to apply spiritual teachings in a real and practical manner. He was able to unify and balance the many opposite forces we discussed in the symbolism of the ladder and leave a living legacy for his children for all time.

Jacob wrestled and defeated the "man," bringing himself a new name and a new identity, one by which the Jewish people and their homeland are called after until this day. His challenges are our challenges, and the Jewish people continue to struggle to fulfill the mission revealed to him on that awesome night, in that awesome place.

## 17

# Following Your Dreams

n Shabbat day, many recite the following verse from Isaiah, describing the reward for guarding the sanctity of the Shabbat: "Then you will be granted pleasure with God and I will cause you to ride on the high places of the earth and feed you with the heritage of Jacob your father" (Isaiah 58:14). Regarding this verse the Talmud states that anyone who has pleasure in Shabbat is granted a portion beyond all boundaries (*Shabbat* 118a). Unlike His promises to Abraham or Isaac, God promised Jacob unlimited boundaries: "Your offspring will be like the dust of the earth and you will spread out to the west, east, north, and south…" (Genesis 28:14).

On the surface it seems contradictory that observing Shabbat, a day when activities are severely restricted, earns us the merit of a portion beyond all boundaries. Yet the restrictions of mundane activities on Shabbat unlock a treasure-house of unlimited spiritual bliss.

This paradox holds true for dreams as well. It would appear at first that a sleep state and loss of consciousness would limit any hope for spiritual advancement. Yet when the shackles are released from the subconscious and the superconscious levels of the soul, we enter a world of limitless possibilities and potential. In this respect dreams, whether in a waking or sleeping state, are beyond all boundaries of time and space.

Each person comes to this world with a mission to accomplish in his or her lifetime. This mission is engraved in the deepest levels of soul. When we dream of how we would like to live our lives and who we would like to become, we are coming in touch with our soul's deepest potential. Our potential is infinite because the soul is a portion of God, who is infinite.

When the soul departs from this world its accomplishments are reviewed by the Heavenly Court. Chassidut explains that even if much good was done and many worthwhile undertakings were accomplished, the Heavenly Court's judgment is based mainly on whether the soul fulfilled the mission for which it came into the world and whether it worked to rectify that which it needed to fix.

The Rebbe of Slonim teaches that we can recognize what we need to rectify by looking at those areas in our lives that are the hardest for us. If specific traits are flawed, certain relationships difficult, and skills or tasks stressful to perform, these are the very areas we need to work on, as they are a sign of what the soul most needs to do to fulfill its mission.

Finding our mission in life is only accomplished through aligning our will with God's will. The methods most conducive to identifying our calling in life are prayer, contemplation, and deep meditation. Daydreaming can also be used if it is purposely directed with the intent of opening oneself to all sorts of possibilities our more logical side would tend to discard.

Many people are so locked into their survival and pleasure instincts they never even seek their true calling in life. Rabbi Shlomo Carlebach tells a beautiful story about Rabbi Naftali Tzvi Yehudah Berlin, known as the "Netziv," who was the head of the Yeshivah of Volozhin. When he published his book *Emek HaDavar*, he made a festive meal and told the following story:

When Rabbi Naftali was a young boy his father, who was a hardworking tailor, wanted him to be a tailor as well. When he was eleven his father began to teach him the trade, but young Naftali knew he didn't really want to be a tailor. One night he had a dream in which he saw himself as a tailor like his father wanted him to be. He was in fact a good tailor. Then he saw that when his years were finished on this earth he went to Heaven. Before he entered the Garden of Eden, though, angels came forth with piles of manuscripts in their hands and said to him, "These are the books you could have written had you gone to study Torah. Look what you've lost!"

In the dream the young Naftali felt a sharp pain and he cried out, "This is what I could have been and instead I was a nice tailor!" He awoke with the pain still deep in his heart. At that moment he decided that if God found him meritorious and allowed him to learn Torah, he would make a great feast whenever he published works of Torah.

Dreaming can be translated into reality, as in the above story, or it can be used as an escape from reality — a comfortable release from the hard work of transforming our dreams into the reality of life. This is why dreams go after their interpretation — ultimately it is our free will to mold our lives however we wish to mold them. Nothing stands before will, especially when trying to make dreams come true.

I heard from Rabbi Shlomo Carlebach the following Chassidic words of wisdom, based on the fact that the root of the Hebrew word for dream, *chalom*, has the same letters as the roots of *lechem*, bread, and *milchamah*, war: Some people fight in order to have bread, while others fight to preserve and manifest their dreams; some eat in order to fight, while others eat in order to dream.

We discussed above the statement in the Talmud that one should wait for at least twenty-two years to see the fulfillment of his dream, as that is how long it took for Joseph's dream to be realized. The Talmud does not say that we can't wait longer, and this applies to an individual as well as to a nation. The Jewish people began dreaming of a rectified world of peace and harmony among all peoples from its very inception. Thousands of years later we are still dreaming of this glorious day. Yet the waiting should not be passive, but rather an ongoing process of drawing the future into the present.

An individual as well has a vision of his or her true self engraved on every level of soul and needs to draw that vision of perfected reality into the present. Dreams and reality are ultimately defined by each individual. May we give our souls permission to dream and then find the strength to make those dreams reality.

# About the Author

Rabbi Avraham Arieh Trugman has been involved in Jewish education for over thirty years. As a founding member of Moshav Meor Modiim in 1976, he went on to be director at the Moshav's Center of Jewish Education, which successfully ran programs for over five thousand participants from over twenty-five countries a year. In 1988 he took the position of regional director of NCSY in Denver, Colorado, where he and his wife created a new region. He returned to Israel in 1995 and currently serves as the director of Ohr Chadash: New Horizons in Jewish Experience, which he founded with his wife.

Rabbi Trugman is the author of *Seeds and Sparks: Inspiration and Self-Expression through the Cycles of Life* (Targum Press, 2003) and *The Mystical Power of Music* (Targum Press, 2005), and he has published articles and poems in a wide variety of publications. He appears at Shabbat programs and lectures extensively worldwide.

# OHR CHADASH

## New Horizons in Jewish Experience

Ohr Chadash is a nonprofit education organization serving English-speaking students enrolled at various universities, yeshivot, seminaries, and long-term programs in Israel, as well as adults, immigrants, and native Israelis. We provide a wide range of programs in an open, joyous, noncoercive, and spiritual atmosphere, where participants are able to explore Judaism at their own pace. Programs include classes, workshops, lunch-and-learn, concerts, Shabbatons, home hospitality, leadership training, seminars, tours, counseling, and social action projects. We combine heart and mind and cater to each participant's special needs. We provide a home away from home for students and visitors and maintain strong relationships for years to come.

Ohr Chadash has run and participated in programs for tens of thousands of people from the full gamut of Jewish backgrounds. With the inspiration and skills that students gain they return to their home communities eager to take leadership roles. Many students and adults return to Israel and the bonds become even stronger. Through our website and e-mail we maintain communication with thousands of alumni and have managed to build a real extended family feeling. As educational follow-up, Ohr Chadash runs and participates in events and programs in cities throughout North America.

Rabbi Avraham Arieh and Rachel Trugman, Directors
Moshav Mevo Modiim, D.N. Hamercaz, Israel, 73122
Tel: 972-8-926-5247 Fax: 972-8-926-5448
E-mail: trugman@netvision.net.il
Website: www.thetrugmans.com.